The Turquo[is]

And, the D[...]

Arthur Cosslett Smith

Alpha Editions

This edition published in 2024

ISBN : 9789362512185

Design and Setting By
Alpha Editions
www.alphaedis.com
Email - info@alphaedis.com

As per information held with us this book is in Public Domain.
This book is a reproduction of an important historical work. Alpha Editions uses the best technology to reproduce historical work in the same manner it was first published to preserve its original nature. Any marks or number seen are left intentionally to preserve its true form.

Contents

THE TURQUOISE CUP ....- 1 -
II ....- 8 -
III ....- 13 -
IV ....- 17 -
V ....- 21 -
VI ....- 27 -
VII ....- 31 -
THE DESERT ....- 36 -
II ....- 40 -
III ....- 42 -
THE MAN WHO KEEPS GOATS ....- 45 -
II ....- 50 -
THE MOTHER OF THE ALMEES ....- 58 -

THE TURQUOISE CUP

The Cardinal Archbishop sat on his shaded balcony, his well-kept hands clasped upon his breast, his feet stretched out so straight before him that the pigeon, perched on the rail of the balcony, might have seen fully six inches of scarlet silk stocking.

The cardinal was a small man, but very neatly made. His hair was as white as spun glass. Perhaps he was sixty; perhaps he was seventy; perhaps he was fifty. His red biretta lay upon a near-by chair. His head bore no tonsure. The razor of the barber and the scythe of Time had passed him by. There was that faint tinge upon his cheeks that comes to those who, having once had black beards, shave twice daily. His features were clearly cut. His skin would have been pallid had it not been olive. A rebellious lock of hair curved upon his forehead. He resembled the first Napoleon, before the latter became famous and fat.

The pigeon's mate came floating through the blue sky that silhouetted the trees in the garden. She made a pretence of alighting upon the balcony railing, sheered off, coquetted among the treetops, came back again, retreated so far that she was merely a white speck against the blue vault, and then, true to her sex, having proved her liberty only to tire of it, with a flight so swift that the eye could scarcely follow her, she came back again and rested upon the farther end of the balcony, where she immediately began to preen herself and to affect an air of nonchalance and virtue.

Her mate lazily opened one eye, which regarded her for a moment, and then closed with a wink.

"Ah, my friends," said the cardinal, "there are days when you make me regret that I am not of the world, but this is not one of them. You have quarrelled, I perceive. When you build your nest down yonder in the cote, I envy you. When you are giving up your lives to feeding your children, I envy you. I watch your flights for food for them. I say to myself, 'I, too, would struggle to keep a child, if I had one. Commerce, invention, speculation—why could I not succeed in one of these? I have arrived in the most intricate profession of all. I am a cardinal archbishop. Could I not have been a stockbroker?' Ah, signore and signora," and he bowed to the pigeons, "you get nearer heaven than we poor mortals. Have you learned nothing—have you heard no whisper—have you no message for me?"

"Your eminence," said a servant who came upon the balcony, a silver tray in his hand, "a visitor."

The cardinal took the card and read it aloud—"The Earl of Vauxhall."

He sat silent a moment, thinking. "I do not know him," he said at length; "but show him up."

He put on his biretta, assumed a more erect attitude, and then turned to the pigeons.

"Adieu," he said; "commercialism approaches in the person of an Englishman. He comes either to buy or to sell. You have nothing in common with him. Fly away to the Piazza, but come back tomorrow. If you do not, I shall miss you sorely."

The curtains parted, and the servant announced, "The Earl of Vauxhall."

The cardinal rose from his chair.

A young man stepped upon the balcony. He was tall and lithe and blond, and six-and-twenty.

"Your grace," he said, "I have come because I am in deep trouble."

"In that event," said the cardinal, "you do me much honor. My vocation is to seek out those who are in trouble. When *they* seek *me* it argues that I am not unknown. You are an Englishman. You may speak your own language. It is not the most flexible, but it is an excellent vehicle for the truth."

"Thank you," said the young man; "that gives me a better chance, since my Italian is of the gondolier type. I speak it mostly with my arms," and he began to gesticulate.

"I understand," said the cardinal, smiling, "and I fear that my English is open to some criticism. I picked it up in the University of Oxford. My friends in the Vatican tell me that it is a patois."

"I dare say," said the young man. "I was at Cambridge."

"Ah," said the cardinal, "how unfortunate. Still, we may be able to understand one another. Will you have some tea? It is a habit I contracted in England, and I find it to be a good one. I sit here at five o'clock, drink my cup of tea, feed the pigeons that light upon the railing, and have a half-hour in which to remember how great is England, and"—with a bow—"how much the rest of the world owes to her."

"A decent sort of chap, for an Italian," thought the earl. The cardinal busied himself with the tea-pot.

"Your grace," said the earl, finally, "I came here in trouble."

"It cannot be of long standing," said the cardinal. "You do not look like one who has passed through the fire."

"No," said the earl, "but I scarcely know what to say to you. I am embarrassed."

"My son," said the cardinal, "when an Englishman is embarrassed he is truly penitent. You may begin as abruptly as you choose. Are you a Catholic?"

"No," replied the earl, "I am of the Church of England."

The cardinal shrugged his shoulders the least bit. "I never cease to admire your countrymen," he said, "On Sundays they say, 'I believe in the Holy Catholic Church,' and, on work-days, they say, 'I believe in the Holy Anglican Church.' You are admirably trained. You adapt yourselves to circumstances."

"Yes," said the earl, a trifle nettled, "I believe we do, but at present I find myself as maladroit as though I had been born on the Continent—in Italy, for example."

"Good," laughed the cardinal; "I am getting to be a garrulous old man. I love to air my English speech, and, in my effort to speak it freely, I sometimes speak it beyond license. Can you forgive me, my lord, and will you tell me how I can serve you?"

"I came," said the Earl of Vauxhall, "to ask you if there is any way in which I can buy the turquoise cup."

"I do not understand," said the cardinal.

"The turquoise cup," repeated the earl. "The one in the treasury of St. Mark's."

The cardinal began to laugh—then he suddenly ceased, looked hard at the earl and asked, "Are you serious, my lord?"

"Very," replied the earl.

"Are you quite well?" asked the cardinal.

"Yes," said the earl, "but I am very uncomfortable."

The cardinal began to pace up and down the balcony.

"My lord," he asked, finally, "have you ever negotiated for the Holy Coat at Treves; for the breastplate of Charlemagne in the Louvre; for the Crown Jewels in the Tower?"

"No," said the earl; "I have no use for them, but I very much need the turquoise cup."

"Are you a professional or an amateur?" asked the cardinal, his eyes flashing, his lips twitching.

"As I understand it," said the earl, slowly, a faint blush stealing into his cheeks, "an 'amateur' is a lover. If that is right, perhaps you had better put me down as an 'amateur.'"

The cardinal saw the blush and his anger vanished.

"Ah," he said, softly, "there is a woman, is there?"

"Yes," replied the earl, "there is a woman."

"Well," said the cardinal, "I am listening."

"It won't bore you?" asked the earl. "If I begin about her I sha'n't know when to stop."

"My lord," said the cardinal, "if there were no women there would be no priests. Our occupation would be gone. There was a time when *men* built churches, beautified them, and went to them. How is it now; even here in Venice, where art still exists, and where there is no bourse? I was speaking with a man only to-day—a man of affairs, one who buys and sells, who has agents in foreign lands and ships on the seas; a man who, in the old religious days, would have given a tenth of all his goods to the Church and would have found honor and contentment in the remainder; but he is bitten with this new-fangled belief of disbelief. He has a sneaking fear that Christianity has been supplanted by electricity and he worships Huxley rather than Christ crucified—Huxley!" and the cardinal threw up his hands. "Did ever a man die the easier because he had grovelled at the knees of Huxley? What did Huxley preach? The doctrine of despair. He was the Pope of protoplasm. He beat his wings against the bars of the unknowable. He set his finite mind the task of solving the infinite. A mere creature, he sought to fathom the mind of his creator. Read the lines upon his tomb, written by his wife—what do they teach? Nothing but 'let us eat and drink, for to-morrow we die.' If a man follows Huxley, then is he a fool if he does not give to this poor squeezed-lemon of a world another twist. If I believed there was nothing after this life, do you think I should be sitting here, feeding the pigeons? Do you think—but there, I have aired my English speech and have had my fling at Huxley. Let me fill your cup and then tell me of this woman whom I have kept waiting all this time by my vanity and my ill manners. Is she English, French, Spanish, or American? There are many Americans nowadays."

"No," said the earl, "she is Irish."

"The most dangerous of all," remarked the cardinal.

"It is plain that you know women," said the earl.

"I?" exclaimed the cardinal. "No; nor any living man."

"Her father." resumed the earl, "was a great brewer in Dublin. He made ripping stout. Perhaps you use it. It has a green label, with a bull's head. He kept straight all through the home-rule troubles, and he chipped in a lot for the Jubilee fund, and they made him Lord Vatsmore. He died two years ago and left one child. She is Lady Nora Daly. She is waiting for me now in the Piazza."

"Perhaps I am detaining you?" said the cardinal.

"By no means," replied the earl. "I don't dare to go back just yet. I met her first at home, last season. I've followed her about like a spaniel ever since. I started in for a lark, and now I'm in for keeps. She has a peculiar way with her," continued the earl, smoothing his hat; "one minute you think you are great chums and, the next, you wonder if you have ever been presented."

"I recognize the Irish variety," said the cardinal.

"She is here with her yacht," continued the earl. "Her aunt is with her. The aunt is a good sort. I am sure you would like her."

"Doubtless," said the cardinal, with a shrug; "but have you nothing more to say about the niece?"

"I followed her here," continued the earl, his hands still busy with his hat, "and I've done my best. Just now, in the Piazza, I asked her to marry me, and she laughed. We went into St. Mark's, and the lights and the music and the pictures and the perfume seemed to soften her. 'Did you mean it?' she said to me. I told her I did. 'Don't speak to me for a little while,' she said, 'I want to think.' That was strange, wasn't it?"

"No," said the cardinal, "I don't think that was strange. I think it was merely feminine."

"We came out of the church," continued the earl, "and I felt sure of her; but when we came into the Piazza and she saw the life of the place, the fountain playing, the banners flying, the pigeons wheeling, and heard the band, she began to laugh and chaff. 'Bobby,' she said, suddenly, 'did you mean it?'

"'Yes,' I said, 'I meant it.' She looked at me for a moment so fixedly that I began to think of the things I had done and which she had not done, of the gulf there was between us—you understand?"

"Yes," said the cardinal, "I understand—that is, I can imagine."

"And then," continued the earl, "I ventured to look into her eyes, and she was laughing at me.

"'Bobby,' she said, 'I believe I've landed you. I know you 're a fortune-hunter, but what blame? I dare say I should be one, but for the beer. I'm throwing myself away. With my fortune and my figure I think I could get a duke, an elderly duke, perhaps, and a little over on his knees, but still a duke. A well-brought-up young woman would take the duke, but I am nothing but a wild Irish girl. Bobby, you are jolly and wholesome, and auntie likes you, and I'll take you—hold hard,' she said, as I moved up—'I'll take you, if you'll give me the turquoise cup.' 'What's that?' I asked. 'The turquoise cup,' she said; 'the one in the treasury of St. Mark's. Give me that and Nora Daly is yours.' 'All right,' I said, 'I'll trot off and buy it.'

"Here I am, your grace, an impecunious but determined man. I have four thousand pounds at Coutts's, all I have in the world; will it lift the cup?"

The cardinal rubbed his white hands together, uncrossed and recrossed his legs, struck the arm of his chair, and burst into a laugh so merry and so prolonged that the earl, perforce, joined him.

"It's funny," said the latter, finally, "but, all the same, it's serious."

"Oh, Love!" exclaimed the cardinal; "you little naked boy with wings and a bow! You give us more trouble than all the rest of the heathen deities combined—you fly about so—you appear in such strange places—you compel mortals to do such remarkable things—you debauch my pigeons, and, when the ill is done, you send your victims to me, or another priest, and ask for absolution, so that they may begin all over again."

"Do I get the cup?" asked the earl, with some impatience.

"My lord," said the cardinal, "if the cup were mine, I have a fancy that I would give it to you, with my blessing and my best wishes; but when you ask me to sell it to you, it is as though you asked your queen to sell you the Kohinoor. She dare not, if she could. She could not, if she dare. Both the diamond and the cup were, doubtless, stolen. The diamond was taken in this century; the cup was looted so long ago that no one knows. A sad attribute of crime is that time softens it. There is a mental statute of limitations that converts possession into ownership. 'We stole the Kohinoor so long ago,' says the Englishman, 'that we own it now.' So it is with the cup. Where did it come from? It is doubtless Byzantine, but where did its maker live; in Byzantium or here, in Venice? We used to kidnap Oriental artists in the good old days when art was a religion. This cup was made by one whom God befriended; by a brain steeped in the love of the beautiful; by a hand so cunning that when it died art languished; by a power so compelling that the treasuries of the world were opened to it. Its bowl is a turquoise, the size and shape of an ostrich's egg, sawn through its longer diameter, and resting on its side. Four gold arms clasp the bowl and meet under it. These arms are set with rubies en cabochon, except one, which is cut in facets. The arms are welded beneath the bowl and form the stem. Midway of the stem, and pierced by it, is a diamond, as large"—the cardinal picked up his teaspoon and looked at it—"yes," he said, "as large as the bowl of this spoon. The foot of the cup is an emerald, flat on the bottom and joined to the stem by a ferrule of transparent enamel. If this treasure were offered for sale the wealth of the world would fight for it. No, no, my lord, you cannot have the cup. Take your four thousand pounds to Testolini, the jeweller, and buy a string of pearls. Very few good women can resist pearls."

"Your grace," said the earl, rising, "I appreciate fully the absurdity of my errand and the kindness of your forbearance. I fear, however, that you scarcely grasp the situation. I am going to marry Lady Nora. I cannot marry her without the cup. You perceive the conclusion—I shall have the cup. Good-by, your grace; I thank you for your patience."

"Good-by," said the cardinal, ringing for a servant. "I wish that I might serve you; but, when children cry for the moon, what is to be done? Come and see me again; I am nearly always at home about this hour."

"I repeat, your grace," said the earl, "that I shall have the cup. All is fair in love and war, is it not?"

There was a certain quality in the earl's voice—that quiet, even note of sincerity which quells riots, which quiets horses, which leads forlorn hopes, and the well-trained ear of the cardinal recognized it.

"Pietro," he said to the servant who answered the bell, "I am going out. My hat and stick. I will go a little way with you, my lord."

They went down the broad stairs together, and the earl noticed, for the first time, that his companion limped.

"Gout?" he asked.

"No," said the cardinal; "the indiscretion of youth. I was with Garibaldi and caught a bullet."

"Take my arm," said the earl.

"Willingly," said the cardinal, "since I know that you will bring me into the presence of a woman worth seeing; a woman who can compel a peer of England to meditate a theft."

"How do you know that?" exclaimed the earl; and he stopped so abruptly that the cardinal put his free hand against his companion's breast to right himself.

"Because," said the cardinal, "I saw your face when you said good-by to me. It was not a pleasant face."

II

They went on silently and soon they came to the Piazza.

"I don't see her," said the earl; "perhaps she has gone back to the church."

They crossed the Piazza and entered St. Mark's.

"Not here," said the earl.

They walked up the south aisle and came to the anteroom of the treasury. Its door was open. They entered what had once been a tower of the old palace. The door of the treasury was also open. They went in and found the sacristan and a woman. She held the turquoise cup in her hands.

"Did you buy it, Bobby?" she exclaimed.

She turned and saw that the earl was not alone.

"Your grace," he said, "I present you to Lady Nora Daly."

She bent with a motion half genuflexion, half courtesy, and then straightened herself, smiling.

The cardinal did not notice the obeisance, but he did notice the smile. It seemed to him, as he looked at her, that the treasures of St. Mark's, the jewelled chalices and patens, the agate and crystal vessels, the reliquaries of gold and precious stones, the candlesticks, the two textus covers of golden cloisonné, and even the turquoise cup itself, turned dull and wan and common by comparison with her beauty.

"Your eminence," she said, "you must pardon Bobby's *gaucherie*. He presented you to me and called you 'your grace.' He forgot, or did not know, that you are a cardinal—a prince—and that I should have been presented to you. Bobby means well, but he is an English peer and a guardsman, so we don't expect much else of Bobby."

"He has done a very gracious thing today," said the cardinal. "He has brought me to you."

Lady Nora looked up quickly, scenting a compliment, and ready to meet it, but the cardinal's face was so grave and so sincere that her readiness forsook her and she stood silent.

The earl seemed to be interested in a crucifix of the eleventh century.

"While my lord is occupied with the crucifix," said the cardinal, "will you not walk with me?"

"Willingly," said Lady Nora, and they went out into the church.

"My dear lady," said the cardinal, after an interval of silence, "you are entering upon life. You have a position, you have wealth, you have youth, you have health, and," with a bow, "you have beauty such as God gives to His creatures only for good purposes. Some women, like Helen of Troy and Cleopatra, have used their beauty for evil. Others, like my Queen, Margarita, and like Mary, Queen of the Scots, have held their beauty as a trust to be exploited for good, as a power to be exercised on the side of the powerless."

"Your eminence," said Lady Nora, "we are now taught in England that Queen Mary was not altogether proper."

"She had beauty, had she not?" asked the cardinal.

"Yes," replied Lady Nora.

"She was beheaded, was she not?" asked the cardinal.

"Yes," said Lady Nora, "and by a very plain woman."

"There you have it!" exclaimed the cardinal. "If Elizabeth had been beautiful and Mary plain, Mary would have kept her head. It is sad to see beautiful women lose their heads. It is sad to see you lose yours."

"Mine?" exclaimed Lady Nora, and she put her hands up to her hat-pins, to reassure herself.

"Yes," said the cardinal, "I fear that it is quite gone."

Lady Nora looked at him with questioning eyes. "Yes," she said, "I must have lost it, for I do not understand you, and I have not always been dull."

"My dear lady," said the cardinal, "the Earl of Vauxhall was good enough to pay me a visit this afternoon."

"Oh," exclaimed Lady Nora, clapping her hands, "if I only could have been behind the curtains! What did he say?"

"He said," replied the cardinal, "that he had asked you to be his wife."

"Indeed he has," said Lady Nora, "and so have others."

"He also said," continued the cardinal, "that you had promised to marry him when he brought you the turquoise cup."

"And so I will," said Lady Nora.

"He proposed to buy the cup," continued the cardinal. "He offered four thousand pounds, which, he said, was all he had in the world."

"Good old Bobby!" exclaimed Lady Nora. "That was nice of him, wasn't it?" and her eyes glistened.

"Yes," said the cardinal, "that was nice of him; but when I had explained how impossible it was to sell the cup he bade me good-by, and, as he was going, said, 'I shall have it. All is fair in love and war.' I feared then that he meant to take the cup. Since I have seen you I am certain of it."

"What larks!" cried Lady Nora. "Fancy Bobby with a dark lantern, a bristly beard, and a red handkerchief about his neck. All burglars are like that, you know; and then fancy him creeping up the aisle with his Johnnie—no, his jimmy—and his felt slippers—fancy Bobby in felt slippers—and he reaches the treasury door, and just then the moon comes up and shines through that window and illuminates the key in St. Peter's hand, and Bobby says, 'An omen,' and he takes out his own key-ring and the first one he tries fits the lock and the door flies open, and Bobby lifts the cup, locks the door, goes down to the steps by the Doge's palace—no gondola—too late, you know, so he puts the cup in his teeth, takes a header, and swims to the yacht. When he comes alongside they hail him, and he comes up the ladder. 'Where's your mistress?' he asks, and they call me, and I come on deck in my pink *saut du lit*, and there stands Bobby, the water running off him and the cup in his teeth. 'There's your bauble,' he says. (Of course he takes the cup out of his mouth when he speaks.) 'And here's your Nora,' I say, and the boatswain pipes all hands aft to witness the marriage ceremony. No, no, your eminence," she laughed, "it's too good to be true. Bobby will never steal the cup. He has never done anything in all his life but walk down Bond Street. He's a love, but he is not energetic."

"You are doubtless right," said the cardinal, "and my fears are but the timidity of age; still—"

The earl joined them. He had just given the sacristan ten pounds, and had endeavored to treat the gift as a disinterested *pourboire*. He felt that he had failed; that he had overdone it, and had made himself a marked man. The sacristan followed him—voluble, eulogistic.

"Tommaso," said the cardinal, "this is the Earl of Vauxhall. He is to have every privilege, every liberty. He is to be left alone if he desires it. He is not to be bothered with attendance or suggestions. He may use a kodak; he may handle anything in the treasury. You will regard him as though he were myself."

Tommaso bowed low. The earl blushed.

Lady Nora looked at her watch.

"Five o'clock!" she exclaimed, "and Aunt Molly will be wanting her tea. The launch is at the stairs. Will you come, Bobby? And you, your eminence, will you honor me?"

"Not to-day, my lady," replied the cardinal, "but perhaps some other."

"To-morrow?" she asked.

"Yes," said the cardinal.

"Thank you," said Lady Nora; "the launch will be at the landing at half-past four."

"Is it an electrical contrivance?" asked the cardinal, with a smile.

"Yes," replied Lady Nora.

"Then," said the cardinal, "you need not send it. I will come in my barca. Electricity and the Church are not friendly. We have only just become reconciled to steam."

Lady Nora laughed. "Good-by," she said, "until to-morrow," and again she made her courtesy.

"Until to-morrow," said the cardinal; and he watched them down the aisle.

"Tommaso," he said to the sacristan, "give me the turquoise cup."

Tommaso handed it to him, silent but wondering.

"Now lock the door," said the cardinal, "and give me the key."

Tommaso complied. The cardinal put the cup under his robe and started down the aisle.

"Tommaso," he said, "you are now closed for the annual cleaning. You understand, do you not?"

"Perfectly, your eminence," replied Tommaso, and then he added—"When a stranger gives me two hundred and fifty lire it is time to lock my door."

The cardinal went out of the church, the turquoise cup under his cassock. He crossed the Piazza slowly, for he was both limping and thinking. He came to the shop of Testolini, the jeweller, under the North arcade, paused a moment, and entered. The clerks behind the counters sprang to their feet and bowed low.

"Signor Testolini?" asked the cardinal; "is he within?"

"Yes, your eminence," said the head clerk. "He is in his bureau. I will summon him."

"No," said the cardinal, "if he is alone I will go in," and he opened the door at the back of the shop and closed it behind him. In ten minutes he came out again. Signor Testolini followed, rubbing his hands and bowing at each step.

"Perfectly, your eminence," he said. "I quite understand."

"It must be in my hands in ten days," said the cardinal.

"Ten days!" exclaimed Testolini; "impossible."

"What is that strange word?" said the cardinal; "it must be a vulgarism of New Italy, that 'impossible.' I do not like it and I will thank you not to use it again when speaking to me. In ten days, Signore."

"Yes, your eminence," said Testolini, "but it will be in the afternoon."

"In ten days," said the cardinal, very quietly.

"Yes, your eminence," said Testolini.

"He looks like Napoleon," whispered the head clerk to his neighbor.

The cardinal went limping down the shop. He had almost reached the door when he stopped and spoke to a little man who stood behind the show-case in which are the enamels.

"Ah, Signore!" he exclaimed, "how come on the wife and baby? I meant to see them this afternoon, but I was diverted. I wish you to continue the same diet for them—take this"—and he fumbled in his pocket, but drew a blank.

"Signor Testolini," he said to the master at his heels, "I find I have no money. Kindly loan me fifty lire. Here," he said to the little man, and he slipped the money into his hand, "plenty of milk for the child;" and he went out of the shop.

"That was not like Napoleon," said the head clerk; and then he added, "Occasionally one meets with a priest who rises superior to his profession."

The little man behind the enamel counter said nothing, but he drew his hand across his eyes.

III

The following day was a busy one for the cardinal. While Pietro was shaving him he parcelled out the hours.

"What time is it, Pietro?" he asked.

"Three minutes past seven, your eminence."

"Good," said the cardinal; "at half-past I make my mass; at eight, I take my coffee; from eight to ten, my poor—by the way, Pietro, is there any money in the house?"

"Yes, your eminence," said Pietro; "there are eight hundred lire in your desk."

"Take fifty of them to Signor Testolini, in the Piazza, with my thanks," said the cardinal, "and put the rest in my purse. Where was I, Pietro?"

"Your eminence had reached ten o'clock," replied Pietro.

"From ten to eleven," continued the cardinal, "audience for the laity; from eleven to half-past, audience for the clergy; half-past eleven, my egg and a salad. Keep all who look hungry, Pietro, and ask them to take *déjeuner* with me; at twelve, see the architect who is restoring the altar-rail at St. Margaret's; take time to write to the Superior at St. Lazzaro in reference to the proof-sheets of the 'Life of Eusebius'; from one to three, my poor—we must get some more money, Pietro; from three to four—"

"There, your eminence!" exclaimed Pietro, "I have cut you."

"Yes," said the cardinal; "I was about to mention it. Where was I?"

"Your eminence was at four o'clock," replied Pietro.

"Four o'clock already!" exclaimed the cardinal, "and nothing done; from four to half-past four, interview with the treasurer of the diocese. That's a bad half-hour, Pietro. At half-past four I wish the barca to be at the landing. Have the men wear their least shabby liveries. I am to visit the English yacht that lies over by St. Giorgio. You must dress me in my best to-day."

"Alas, your eminence," said Pietro, "your best cassock is two years old."

"How old is the one I wore yesterday?" asked the cardinal.

"Four years at least," said Pietro. "You have your ceremonial dress, but nothing better for the street."

"I caught a glimpse of myself in one of Testolini's mirrors yesterday," said the cardinal, "and I thought I looked rather well."

"Your eminence," said Pietro, "you saw your face and not your coat."

"Pietro," said the cardinal, rising, "you should have turned your hand to diplomacy; you would have gone far."

At half-past four o'clock the cardinal's barca drew up to the molo. The oarsmen were dressed in black, save that their sashes and stockings were scarlet. The bowman landed. It was as though a footman came off the box of a brougham and waited on the curb. While the figures on the clock-tower were still striking the half-hour, the cardinal came limping across the Piazza. The gondoliers at the molo took off their hats and drew up in two lines. The cardinal passed between them, looking each man in the face. He beckoned to one, who left the ranks and came up to him, awkward and sheepish.

"Emilio," said the cardinal, "I have arranged your matter. You are to pay four lire a week, and are to keep out of the wine-shops. Mind, now, no drinking." To another he said, "I have looked into your case, Marco. You are perfectly right. I have employed counsel for you. Attend to your business and forget your trouble. It is my trouble, now." To a man to whom he beckoned next he spoke differently. "How dare you send me such a petition?" he exclaimed. "It was false from beginning to end. You never served in the legion. The woman you complain of is your lawful wife. You married her in Padua ten years ago. You have been imprisoned for petit theft. You got your gondolier's license by false pretences. Mark you, friends," he said, turning, "here is one of your mates who will bear watching. When he slips, come to me," and he stepped into his barca.

"To the English yacht," he said.

When they arrived they found the Tara dressed in flags, from truck to deck; Lady Nora stood on the platform of the boarding-stairs, and the crew were mustered amidships.

"Your eminence," cried Lady Nora, "you should have a salute if I knew the proper number of guns."

"My dear lady," said the cardinal, taking off his hat, "the Church militant does not burn gunpowder, it fights hand to hand. Come for me at six," he said to his poppe.

"Surely," said Lady Nora, "you will dine with us. We have ices with the Papal colors, and we have a little box for Peter's pence, to be passed with the coffee. I shall be much disappointed if you do not dine with us."

"Wait!" called the cardinal to his barca. The oarsmen put about. "Tell Pietro," he said, "to feed the pigeons as usual. Tell him to lay crumbs on the balcony railing, and if the cock bird is too greedy, to drive him away and give the hen an opportunity. Come for me at nine."

"Thank you," said Lady Nora; "your poor are now provided for."

"Alas, no," said the cardinal; "my pigeons are my aristocratic acquaintance. They would leave me if I did not feed them. My real poor have two legs, like the pigeons, but God gave them no feathers. They are the misbegotten, the maladroit, the unlucky,—I stand by that word,— the halt, the blind, those with consciences too tender to make their way, reduced gentlefolk, those who have given their lives for the public good and are now forgotten, all these are my poor, and they honor me by their acquaintance. My pigeons fly to my balcony. My poor never come near me. I am obliged, humbly, to go to them."

"Will money help?" exclaimed Lady Nora; "I have a balance at my banker's."

"No, no, my lady," said the cardinal; "money can no more buy off poverty than it can buy off the bubonic plague. Both are diseases. God sent them and He alone can abate them. At His next coming there will be strange sights. Some princes and some poor men will be astonished."

Just then, a woman, short, plump, red-cheeked and smiling, came toward them. She was no longer young, but she did not know it.

"Your eminence," said Lady Nora, "I present my aunt, Miss O'Kelly."

Miss O'Kelly sank so low that her skirts made what children call "a cheese" on the white deck.

"Your imminence," she said, slowly rising, "sure this is the proud day for Nora, the Tara, and meself."

"And for me, also," said the cardinal. "From now until nine o'clock I shall air my English speech, and I shall have two amiable and friendly critics to correct my mistakes."

"Ah, your imminence," laughed Miss O'Kelly, "I don't speak English. I speak County Clare."

"County Clare!" exclaimed the cardinal; "then you know Ennis? Fifty odd years ago there was a house, just out of the town of Ennis, with iron gates and a porter's lodge. The Blakes lived there."

"I was born in that house," said Miss O'Kelly. "It was draughty, but it always held a warm welcome."

"I do not remember the draught," said the cardinal, "but I do remember the welcome. When I was an undergraduate at Oxford, I made a little tour of Ireland, during a long vacation. I had letters from Rome. One of them was to the chapter at Ennis. A young priest took me to that house. I went back many times. There was a daughter and there were several strapping sons. The boys did nothing, that I could discover, but hunt and shoot. They were amiable, however. The daughter hunted, also, but she did many other things. She kept the house, she visited the poor, she sang Irish songs to perfection, and she flirted beyond compare. She had hair so black that I can give you no notion of its sheen; and eyes as blue as our Venetian skies. Her name was Nora—Nora Blake. She was the most beautiful woman I had ever seen—until yesterday."

"She was my mother!" exclaimed Miss O'Kelly.

"And my grandmother," said Lady Nora.

The cardinal drew a breath so sharp that it was almost a sob, then he took Lady Nora's hand.

"My child," he said, "I am an old man. I am threescore years and ten, and six more, and you bring back to me the happiest days of my youth. You are the image of Nora Blake, yes, her very image. I kiss the images of saints every day," he added, "why not this one?" and he bent and kissed Lady Nora's hand.

There was so much solemnity in the act that an awkward pause might have followed it had not Miss O'Kelly been Irish.

"Your imminence," she said, "since you've told us your age, I'll tell you mine. I'm two-and-twenty and I'm mighty tired of standin'. Let's go aft and have our tay."

They had taken but a few steps when Lady Nora, noticing the cardinal's limp, drew his arm through her own and supported him.

"I know the whole story," she whispered. "You loved my grandmother."

"Yes," said the cardinal, "but I was unworthy."

IV

They had their tea, two white-clad stewards serving them. The cardinal took a second cup and then rose and went to the side. He crumbled a biscuit along the rail.

"I have often wondered," he said, "if my pigeons come for me or for my crumbs. Nora Blake used to say that her poor were as glad to see her without a basket as with one. But she was a saint. She saw things more clearly than it is given to us to see them."

The women looked at each other, in silence.

"No," said the cardinal, after an interval, "they do not come; they are as satisfied with Pietro's crumbs as with mine. Love is not a matter of the stomach;" and he brushed the crumbs overboard. "Perhaps the fishes will get them," he added, "and they will not know whence they came. Anonymous charity," he continued, coming back to his chair, "is the best. It curbs the pride of the giver and preserves the pride of the recipient. Open giving is becoming a trade. It is an American invention. Very rich men in that country offer so much for an object—a college—a hospital—a library—if some one else will give so much. The offer is printed in the newspapers of the land and its originator reaps much—what is the word I wish?—acclaim? no; kudos? no;—ah, yes, advertisement; that is the word. Thank God that charity does not thus masquerade in Italy. There are men here, in poor old Venice, who give half their goods to feed the poor. Are their names published? No. The newspapers reason thus—'Here is a gentleman; let us treat him as one,' We have no professional philanthropists in Italy. After all," he added, "mere giving is the lowest form of charity. If all the wealth of the world were divided the world would be debauched. Binding up wounds, pouring in oil and wine, bringing the wronged man to an inn, giving him your companionship, your sympathy, so that he shows his heart to you and lets you heal its bruises—that is your true charity."

"That's what I'm telling Nora," exclaimed Miss O'Kelly; "she's forever drawing checks. There was my nephew, Nora's cousin, Phelim. He gave away all he had. He gave it to the piquet players in the Kildare Club. 'Aunt Molly,' he said to me, 'piquet has cost me fifteen thousand pounds, and I am just beginning to learn the game. Now that I know it a bit, no one will play with me. Your bread cast on the waters may come back, but it's ten to one it comes back mouldy, from the voyage.' Phelim is the flower of the family, your imminence. He is six foot three. He was out twice before he was two-and-twenty. The first time was with Liftennant Doyle of the Enniskillens. 'Twas about a slip of a girl that they both fancied. The Liftennant fired at the word and missed. 'Try your second barrel,' called Phelim, 'I'm still within bounds' (that's pigeon-shootin' talk, your imminence). The Liftennant laughed and the two went off to the club, arm in arm, and they stayed there two days. There's waiters in the club yet, that remembers it. The next time Phelim was out, 'twas with a little attorney-man from Cork, named Crawford. There was no girl this time; 'twas more serious; 'twas about a horse Phelim had sold, and the little attorney-man had served a writ, and Phelim went down to Cork and pulled the little man's nose. Whin the word was given the attorney-man fired and nicked Phelim's ear. Phelim raised his pistol, slow as married life, and covered the little man. 'Take off your hat!' called Phelim. The little man obeyed, white as paper, and shakin' like a leaf. 'Was the horse sound?' called Phelim. 'He was,' said the little man 'Was he six years old?' called Phelim. 'At least,' said the little man. 'None of your quibbles,' called Phelim. 'He was six, to a minute,' said the little man, looking into the pistol, 'Was he chape at the price?' asked Phelim. 'He was a gift,' said the attorney 'Gentlemen,' says Phelim, 'you have heard this dyin' confession—we will now seal it,' and he sent a bullet through the attorney-man's hat. I had it all from Dr. Clancey, who was out with them. They sent Phelim to Parliament after that, but he took the Chiltern Hundreds and came home. He said his duties interfered with the snipe-shootin'. You'd like Phelim, your imminence."

"I am sure I should," said the cardinal.

"He's in love with Nora," said Miss O'Kelly.

"Ah," said the cardinal, "I spoke too quickly."

Meanwhile the shadows began to creep across the deck. The cardinal rose from his chair.

"At what hour do you dine?" he asked.

"I made the hour early when I heard you order your barca for nine," said Lady Nora; "I said half-past seven."

"Then," said the cardinal, "I should excuse you, but I do it reluctantly. I am keeping you from your toilet."

Miss O'Kelly laughed. "Your imminence," she said, "when a woman reaches my age it takes her some time to dress. I told you I was two-and-twenty. It will take my maid nearly an hour to make me look it," and, with a courtesy, she went below.

Lady Nora stayed behind. "Your eminence," she said, "the evening will be fine; shall we dine on deck?"

"That will be charming," said the cardinal.

"Whenever you wish to go to your room," said Lady Nora, "you have but to press this button, and the head steward will come." She still loitered. "I think it very likely," she said, hesitating, "that the Earl of Vauxhall will drop in; he often does. I should have mentioned it before, but I was so delighted at your staying that I forgot all about him."

"My dear lady," said the cardinal, "to supplant the Earl of Vauxhall in your thoughts is great honor."

She looked at him quickly, blushed, cast down her eyes, and began, nervously, to play with a gold boat-whistle that hung at her belt. When she had exhausted the possibilities of the whistle she looked up again, and the cardinal saw that there were tears upon her cheeks. When she knew that he had seen them she disregarded them, and threw up her head, proudly.

"Yes," she said, "I think of him far too often; so often that it makes me angry, it makes me ashamed. He is an earl; he is tall and straight and beautiful and clean, and—he loves me—I know it," she exclaimed, her face illumined; "but why," she went on, "should I give myself to him on these accounts? Why should he not earn me? Why does he compel me to so one-sided a bargain? I, too, am tall and straight and clean, and not ill-favored, and, in addition, I have that curse of unmarried women—I have money. Why does he not *do* something to even up the transaction? Why does he not write a page that some one will read? Why does he not write a song that some one will sing? Why does he not do something that will make the world call me his wife, instead of calling him my husband? The other day, when he and love were tugging at me, I told him I would marry him if he brought me the turquoise cup. It was an idle thing to say, but what I say I stand by. I shall never marry him unless he brings it to me. You know us Irish women. We have our hearts to contend with, but we keep our word. I set my lord a trivial task. If he really wants me he will accomplish it. I am not dear at the price."

"With true love," said the cardinal, "I do not think there is any question of price. It is an absolute surrender, without terms. I say this guardedly, for I am no expert as to this thing called human love. I recognize that it is the power that moves the world, but, for more than fifty years, I have tried to forget the world."

"Yes," cried Lady Nora, "and, but for a cruel mistake, you would have married my grandmother."

"Yes," said the cardinal, "but for a cruel mistake."

"The mistake was hers," exclaimed Lady Nora.

The cardinal threw up his hands. "It was a mistake," he said, "and it was buried fifty years ago. Why dig it up?"

"Forgive me," said Lady Nora, and she started toward the hatch.

"My child," said the cardinal, "you say that you will not marry his lordship unless he brings you the cup. Do you hope that he will bring it?"

She looked at him a moment, the red and white roses warring in her cheeks. "Yes," she said, "I hope it, for I love him," and she put her hands to her face and ran below.

"If the earl is the man I take him to be," said the cardinal to himself, "I fear that I am about to shut my eyes to a felony," and he pressed the electric button at his side. The head steward appeared so quickly that he overheard the cardinal say—"I certainly should have done it, at his age."

V

At six bells there was a tap on the cardinal's door.

"Come in," he said.

The head steward entered. He had exchanged the white duck of the afternoon for the black of evening. He was now the major-domo. He wore silk stockings and about his neck was a silver chain, and at the end of the chain hung a key.

"Your eminence's servant has come on board," he said.

"Pietro?" asked the cardinal.

"I do not know his name," said the steward, "but he is most anxious to see your eminence."

"Let him come in at once," said the cardinal. The steward backed out, bowing.

There was a loud knock upon the door. "Enter," said the cardinal. Pietro came in. He carried a portmanteau.

"What is it?" exclaimed the cardinal. "Is any one dying? Am I needed?"

"No, your eminence," said Pietro, "the public health is unusually good. I have come to dress you for dinner with the English."

"They are not English," said the cardinal; "they are Irish."

"In that event," said Pietro, "you will do as you are."

"No," laughed the cardinal, "since you have brought my finery I will put it on."

Pietro opened the portmanteau with a sigh. "I thought they were English," he said. "The Irish are as poor as the Italians. If I dress your eminence as I had intended they will not appreciate it."

"Do not fear," said the cardinal. "Do your best."

At seven bells there was another knock at the cardinal's door. Pietro opened it.

"Shall dinner be served, your eminence?" asked the head steward.

"Whenever the ladies are ready," replied the cardinal.

"They are already on deck, your eminence."

"At once, then," said the cardinal, and he went up the companion-way, leaning on Pietro's arm. The after-deck was lighted by scores of incandescent lamps, each shaded by a scarlet silken flower. The table stood, white and cool, glittering with silver and crystal. In its centre was a golden vase, and in the vase were four scarlet roses. The deck was covered with a scarlet carpet, a strip of which ran forward to the galley-hatch, so that the service might be noiseless.

Lady Nora was dressed in white and wore no jewels. Miss O'Kelly was partially clad in a brocaded gown, cut as low as even the indiscretion of age permits. A necklace of huge yellow topazes emphasized the space they failed to cover.

The cardinal came into the glow of the lights. His cassock was black, but its hem, its buttons, and the pipings of its seams were scarlet; so were his stockings; so was the broad silk sash that circled his waist; so were the silk gloves, thrust under the sash; so was the birettina, the little skullcap that barely covered his crown and left to view a fringe of white hair and the rebellious lock upon his forehead. The lace at his wrists was Venice point. His pectoral cross was an antique that would grace the Louvre. Pietro had done his work well.

The cardinal came into the zone of light, smiling. "Lady Nora," he said. "Ireland is the home of the fairies. When I was there I heard much of them. Early in the morning I saw rings in the dew-laden grass and was told that they had been made by the 'little people,' dancing. You, evidently, have caught a fairy prince and he does your bidding. Within an hour you have converted the after-deck into fairy-land; you have—"

Just then, out of the blue darkness that lay between the yacht and Venice, burst the lights of a gondola. They darted alongside and, a moment after, the Earl of Vauxhall came down the deck.

"Serve at once," whispered Lady Nora to the major-domo.

"Pardon me, your eminence," she said, "you were saying—"

"I was merely remarking," said the cardinal, "that you seem to have a fairy prince ready to do your bidding. It seems that I was right. Here he is."

Lady Nora smiled. "What kept you, Bobby," she said, "a business engagement, or did you fall asleep?"

"Neither," said the earl; "I lost a shirt-stud."

"Your eminence is served," said the major-domo.

They stood while the cardinal said grace, at the conclusion of which, all, except the earl, crossed themselves.

"Was it a valuable jewel, my lord?" asked Miss O'Kelly, in an interval of her soup.

"No," said the earl; "a poor thing, but mine own."

"How did it happen?" asked Miss O'Kelly; "did your man stale it?"

"Dear, no," said the earl; "it happened while I was putting on my shirt."

Miss O'Kelly blushed, mentally, and raised her napkin to her face.

"It twisted out of my fingers," continued the earl, "and rolled away, somewhere. I moved every piece of furniture in the room; I got down on all fours and squinted along the floor; I went to the dressing-table to look for another; my man, after putting out my things, had locked up everything and gone to his dinner. I couldn't dine with you, like freedom, 'with my bosom bare'—"

"No," said Miss O'Kelly, glancing down at her topazes, "you couldn't do that."

"Certainly not," said the earl, "and so I put on my top-coat and went out to Testonni's in the Piazza, and bought a stud. I was lucky to find them open, for it was past closing time. They told me they were working late on a hurry order. I put the stud in my shirt, raced across to the molo, jumped into a gondola, and here I am. Am I forgiven?"

"Yes," said Lady Nora; "you were only five minutes late and your excuse is, at least, ingenious. You could not have come unadorned."

"Unadorned!" exclaimed the earl; "it was a question of coming unfastened."

Pietro began to refill the cardinal's glass, but his master stopped him. Pietro bent and whispered. The cardinal laughed. "Pietro tells me," he said, "that this is better wine than that which I get at home and that I should make the most of it. The only difference I remark in wines is that some are red and some are white."

"That minds me of one night when Father Flynn dropped in to dine," said Miss O'Kelly—"'twas he had the wooden leg, you remember, Nora, dear—and he and Phelim sat so late that I wint in with fresh candles. 'I call that good whiskey,' says the father as I came in. '*Good* whiskey?' exclaimed Phelim; 'did ever you see any whiskey that was *bad*.' 'Now that you mintion it,' says his riverince, 'I never did; but I've seen some that was scarce.' 'Another bottle, Aunt Molly,' says Phelim, 'his riverince has a hollow leg.' When I came back with the bottle they were talking to a little, wild gossoon from the hills. He was barefooted, bareheaded, and only one suspinder was between him and the police. 'Is your mother bad?' asked his riverince. 'Dochtor says she'll die afore mornin',' says the gossoon. 'Will you lind me a horse, Phelim?' asked his riverince. 'You ride a horse, with that leg!' says Phelim. 'No, I'll drive you, in the cart;' and he went off to the stables. In five minutes he came back with the dog-cart and the gray mare. His riverince got up, with the aid of a chair, the little gossoon climbed up behind, and the gravel flew as the gray mare started. They wint a matter of ten rods and then I saw the lamps again. They had turned, and they stopped before the porch—the gray mare on her haunches. 'Phelim,' I says, 'what ails you, you've a light hand whin you're sober.' His riverince leaned over and whispered—'The oil cruet, Miss Molly, and don't let the gossoon see it,' I wint in, came out with the cruet in a paper, and handed it to him. 'All right, Phelim,' he says, and the gray mare started. At six in the mornin' I heard the gravel crunch, and I wint to the door. There stood the gray mare, her head down, and her tail bobbin'. 'You've over-driven her, Phelim,' says I. 'Perhaps,' says he, 'but I knew you were sittin' up for me. The curse of Ireland,' says he, 'is that her women sit up for her men.' 'How is the poor woman?' I says. 'She's dead,' says Phelim; 'Father Flynn is waiting for the neighbors to come.' 'And the little gossoon?' says I. Phelim leaned down from the dog-cart; 'Aunt Molly,' says he, 'we can't afford to keep what we have already, can we?' 'No,' says I. 'Thin,' says Phelim, 'we can just as well afford to keep one more; so I told him to come to us, after the funeral.'"

"I don't quite follow that reasoning," said the earl.

"I am more sure than ever, that I should like Phelim," said the cardinal. "Why do you not have him on?"

"He's six foot three," explained Miss O'Kelly; "the yacht wouldn't fit him. He couldn't stand up, below. There is six foot seven between decks, but the electric lights project four inches. Then the beds—there isn't one more than six foot six. We had Phelim on board and tried him. He stayed one night. 'Aunt Molly,' he said, in the mornin', 'Nora has a beautiful boat, plenty of towels, and a good cook. I should like to go with you, but I'm scared. I kept awake last night, with my knees drawn up, and all went well, but if ever I fall asleep and straighten out, I'll kick the rudder out of her.' We couldn't have Phelim aboard, your imminence; he'd cancel the marine insurance."

While Miss O'Kelly had been running on, the cardinal had been politely listening. He had also been discreetly observing. He had the attribute of politicians and ecclesiastics—he could exercise all his senses together. While he was smiling at Miss O'Kelly he had seen Lady Nora take from the gold vase one of the scarlet roses, press it, for an instant, to her lips and then, under cover of the table, pass it to the earl. He had seen the earl slowly lift the rose to his face, feigning to scent it while he kissed it. He had seen quick glances, quivering lips that half-whispered, half-kissed; he had seen the wireless telegraphy of love flashing messages which youth thinks are in cipher, known only to the sender and the recipient; and he, while laughing, had tapped the wire and read the correspondence.

"It is all over," he said to himself. "They are in love. The little naked boy with the bow has hit them both."

Promptly at nine, Pietro announced the barca. The cardinal made his adieus. "My lord," he said to the earl, "if you are for the shore, I should be honored by your company."

"Thank you," said the earl, "but I ordered my gondola at ten."

Lady Nora and the earl stood watching the cardinal's lantern as it sped toward Venice. It was soon lost in the night. Lady Nora's hand rested upon the rail. The earl covered it with his own. She did not move.

"Have you bought the cup, Bobby," she asked.

"Not yet," he answered, "but I shall have it. The treasury is closed for the annual cleaning."

"When you bring it," she said, "you will find me here. I should like you to give it me on the Tara. There is your gondola light. Aunt Molly seems to be asleep in her chair. You need not wake her to say good-night."

"I sha'n't," said the earl.

Her hand still rested upon the rail—his hand still covered hers. She was gazing across the harbor at the countless lights of Venice. The warm night breeze from the lagoon dimpled the waters of the harbor until the reflected lights began to tremble. There was no sound, save the tinkle of the water against the side and the faint cry of a gondolier, in the distance.

"Bobby," said Lady Nora, finally, "it is nice to be here, just you and I."

He made a quick motion to take her in his arms, but she started back. "No, no," she said, "not yet; not till you earn me. There may be many a slip 'twixt the cup and"—she put her fingers to her lips.

Miss O'Kelly's chin fell upon her topazes so sharply that she wakened with a start.

"Nora, darlin'?" she cried, looking about her.

"Here I am," said Lady Nora, coming into the light.

"Ah," said her aunt, "and Lord Robert, too. I thought he had gone. I must have had forty winks."

"I was only waiting," said the earl, "to bid you good-night."

"An Irishman," said Miss O'Kelly, "would have taken advantage of me slumbers, and would have kissed me hand."

"An Englishman will do it when you are awake," said the earl.

"That's nice," said Miss O'Kelly; "run away home now, and get your beauty-sleep."

VI

During the following week the cardinal was so occupied with his poor that he nearly forgot his rich. He saw the yacht whenever he took his barca at the molo, and once, when he was crossing the Rialto, he caught a glimpse of Lady Nora and her aunt, coming up the canal in their gondola.

As for the earl, he haunted St. Mark's. Many times each day he went to the treasury only to find it locked. The sacristan could give him no comfort. "Perhaps to-morrow, my lord," he would say when the earl put his customary question; "it is the annual cleaning, and sometimes a jewel needs resetting, an embroidery to be repaired—all this takes time—perhaps to-morrow. Shall I uncover the Palo d'Oro, my Lord, or light up the alabaster column; they are both very fine?" And the earl would turn on his heel and leave the church, only to come back in an hour to repeat his question and receive his answer.

One day the earl spoke out—"Tommaso," he said, "you are not a rich man, I take it?"

"My lord," replied Tommaso, "I am inordinately poor. Are you about to tempt me?"

The earl hesitated, blushed, and fumbled in his pocket. He drew out a handful of notes.

"Take these," he said, "and open the treasury."

"Alas, my lord," said Tommaso, "my virtue is but a battered thing, but I must keep it. I have no key."

The earl went out and wandered through the arcades. He came upon Lady Nora and Miss O'Kelly. They were looking at Testolini's shop-windows. Lady Nora greeted him with a nod—Miss O'Kelly with animation.

"I'm havin' a struggle with me conscience," she said.

So was the earl.

"Do ye see that buttherfly?" continued Miss O'Kelly, putting her finger against the glass; "it's marked two hundred lire, and that's eight pounds. I priced one in Dublin, just like it, and it was three hundred pounds. They don't know the value of diamonds in Italy. I've ten pounds that I got from Phelim yesterday, in a letther. He says there's been an Englishman at the Kildare Club for three weeks, who thought he could play piquet. Phelim is travellin' on the Continent. Now, the question in me mind is, shall I pay Father Flynn the ten pounds I promised him, a year ago Easter, or shall I buy the buttherfly? It would look illigant, Nora, dear, with me blue bengaline."

Lady Nora laughed, "I am sure, Aunt Molly," she said, "that Phelim would rather you bought the butterfly, I'll take care of your subscription to Father Flynn."

With an exclamation of joy, Miss O'Kelly ran into the shop.

"Nora," said the earl, "the treasury is still closed."

"Oh," said Lady Nora, "why do you remind me of such tiresome things as the treasury? Didn't you hear Aunt Molly say that Phelim is on the Continent? I had a wire from him this morning. Read it; it's quite Irish."

She handed the earl a telegram.

"Shall I read it?" he asked.

"Of course," she answered.

He read—"*I'm richer, but no shorter. Is there a hotel in Venice big enough to take me in? Wire answer.* PHELIM."

"Will you send this reply for me?" she asked, when the earl had read Phelim's telegram.

"To be sure I will," he said.

"How many words are there?" she asked. "I'll pay for it."

Thus compelled, the earl read her answer—"*Come, rich or poor, long or short. Come.* NORA."

The earl went off with the telegram, thinking.

The next afternoon the earl came out of the church—his fifth visit since ten o'clock—and there, near the fountain, were Lady Nora and her aunt. The earl marked them from the church steps. There was no mistaking Miss O'Kelly's green parasol.

This time Lady Nora met him with animation. She even came toward him, her face wreathed in smiles.

"Phelim has come!" she exclaimed.

"Quite happy—I'm sure," said the earl. "He's prompt, isn't he?"

"Yes," said Lady Nora, "he's always prompt. He doesn't lose shirt-studs, and he never dawdles."

"Ah!" said the earl.

"Here he comes!" exclaimed Lady Nora, and she began to wave her handkerchief.

The earl turned and saw, coming from the corner by the clock-tower, a man. He had the shoulders of Hercules, the waist of Apollo, the legs of Mercury. When he came closer, hat in hand, the earl saw that he had curling chestnut locks, a beard that caressed his chin, brown eyes, and white teeth, for he was smiling.

"Nora," he cried, as he came within distance, "your friend the cardinal is a good one. He puts on no side. He had me up on the balcony, opened your letter, took out the check, and read the letter before even he looked at the stamped paper. When a man gets a check in a letter and reads the letter before he looks at the check, he shows breedin'."

"The Earl of Vauxhall," said Lady Nora, "I present Mr. Phelim Blake."

The two men nodded; the earl, guardedly; Phelim, with a smile.

"I think, my lord," said Phelim, "that you are not in Venice for her antiquities. No more am I. I arrived this mornin' and I've been all over the place already. I was just thinkin' that time might hang. Twice a day I've to go out to the yacht to propose to Nora. Durin' the intervals we might have a crack at piquet."

The earl was embarrassed. He was not accustomed to such frankness. He was embarrassed also by the six feet three of Phelim. He himself was only six feet.

"I do not know piquet," he said.

"Ah," said Phelim, "it cost me much to learn what I know of it, and I will gladly impart that little for the pleasure of your companionship. I will play you for love."

The earl took counsel with himself—"So long as he is playing piquet with me," he said to himself, "so long he cannot be making love to Nora."

"How long will it take me to learn the game?" he asked.

"As long," answered Phelim, "as you have ready money. When you begin to give due bills you have begun to grasp the rudiments of the game."

"Then," said the earl, "I shall be an apt pupil, for I shall give an IOU the first time I lose"

"In piquet," said Phelim, squaring himself, and placing the index finger of his right hand in his left hand, after the manner of the didactic, "the great thing is the discard, and your discard should be governed by two considerations— first, to better your own hand, and second, to cripple your opponent's. Your moderate player never thinks of this latter consideration. His only thought is to better his own hand. He never discards an ace. The mere size of it dazzles him, and he will keep aces and discard tens, forgetting that you cannot have a sequence of more than four without a ten, and that you can have one of seven without the ace, and that a king is as good as an ace, if the latter is in the discard. I am speakin' now," continued Phelim, "of the beginner. Let us suppose one who has spent one thousand pounds on the game, and is presumed to have learned somethin' for his money. His fault is apt to be that he sacrifices too much that he may count cards. I grant you that you cannot count sixty or ninety if your opponent has cards, but you may, if cards are tied. When I was a beginner I used to see Colonel Mellish make discards, on the mere chance of tyin' the cards, that seemed to me simply reckless. I soon discovered, however, that they were simply scientific. One more thing—always remember that there is no average card in a piquet pack. The average is halfway between the ten-spot and the knave. Now, what are the chances of the junior hand discardin' a ten and drawin' a higher card? In the Kildare Club they are understood to be two and three-eighths to one against, although Colonel Mellish claims they are two and five-eighths to one. The colonel is an authority, but I think he is a trifle pessimistic. He—"

"There, Phelim," said Lady Nora, "I think that is enough for the first lesson. We dine at eight. If Lord Vauxhall has nothing better to do perhaps he will come with you."

"We'll dine on deck, Phelim, dear," said Miss O'Kelly. "You won't have to go below."

VII

The next morning the earl went to the church, as usual. He had not slept well. The advent of Phelim had set him to thinking. Here was a rival; and a dangerous one. He admitted this grudgingly, for an Englishman is slow to see a rival in a foreigner, and who so foreign as an Irishman?

At dinner, on the yacht, the night before, Phelim had been much in evidence. His six feet three had impressed the earl's six feet. Phelim had been well dressed. "Confound him," thought the earl, "he goes to Poole, or Johns & Pegg. Why doesn't he get his clothes at home?" Then Phelim had talked much, and he had talked well. He had told stories at which the earl had been compelled to laugh. He had related experiences of his home-life, of the peasants, the priests, the clubs, hunting and shooting, his brief stay in Parliament, what he had seen in Venice during the last few days; and, when dinner was over, Lady Nora, who had been all attention, said: "Sing for us, Phelim," and they had gone below, Phelim stooping to save his head; and he had struck those mysterious chords upon the piano, by way of prelude, that silence talk, that put the world far away, that set the men to glancing at the women, and the women to glancing at the floor and making sure of their handkerchiefs, and then—he had sung.

How can one describe a song? As well attempt to paint a perfume.

When Phelim finished singing Miss O'Kelly went over and kissed him, and Lady Nora went away, her eyes glistening.

The earl remembered all these things as he went up the aisle. He had passed that way five times each day for nine days. He came to the door of the treasury, thinking, not of Nora, but of Phelim—and the door was open.

He went in. The gorgeous color of the place stopped him, on the threshold. He saw the broidered vestments upon which gold was the mere background; jacinths were the stamens of the flowers, and pierced diamonds were the dewdrops on their leaves; he saw the chalices and patens of amethyst and jade, the crucifixes of beaten gold, in which rubies were set solid, as if they had been floated on the molten metal; he saw the seven-light candelabrum, the bobèches of which were sliced emeralds, and then his eyes, groping in this wilderness of beauty, lighted on the turquoise cup.

"My God!" he exclaimed, "she is right. She is selling herself for the most beautiful thing in the world. To steal it is a crime like Cromwell's—too great to be punished," and he put out his hand.

Then, with the cup and Nora within his reach, he heard a still, small voice, and his hand fell.

He began to argue with his conscience. "Who owns this cup?" he asked. "No one. The cardinal said it had been stolen. He said no one could sell it because no one could give title. Why, then, is it not mine as well as any one's? If I take it, whom do I wrong? Great men have never let trifles of right and wrong disturb their conduct. Who would ever have won a battle if he had taken thought of the widows? Who would ever have attained any great thing if he had not despised small things?" and he put out his hand again; and then came surging into his mind the provisions of that code which birth, associations, his school life, and, most of all, his mother, had taught him. What would they say and do at his clubs? Where, in all the world, could he hide himself, if he did this thing? He turned and fled, and, running down the church steps, he came face to face with Lady Nora and Phelim. They were laughing gayly; but, when they saw the earl's face, their laughter ceased.

"Have you seen a ghost, my lord?" asked Phelim.

The earl did not answer; he did not even hear. He stood gazing at Lady Nora. For one brief moment, when he stood before the cup, he had questioned whether a woman who would impose such a condition could be worth winning; and now, before her, her beauty overwhelmed him. He forgot Phelim; he forgot the passers-by; he forgot everything, except the woman he loved—the woman he had lost.

"Nora," he said, "I give you back your promise. I cannot give you the cup."

The color left her cheeks and her hands flew up to her heart—she gazed at him with love and pity in her eyes, and then, suddenly, her cheeks flamed, her white teeth pressed her lower lip, her little foot stamped upon the pavement.

"Very well," she said, "I regret having given you so much trouble;" and she went toward the landing. She took three steps and then turned. The two men stood as she had left them.

"Phelim," she said, smiling, "*you* would do something for me, if I were to ask you, would you not?"

"Try me," said Phelim. "Would you like the Campanile for a paper-weight?"

"No," she said, "not that, but something else. Come here."

He went to her, and she whispered in his ear.

"I'll bring it you in half an hour, aboard the yacht," said Phelim, and he started across the Piazza.

Lady Nora went on toward the landing. The earl stood watching her. She did not look back. The earl looked up at the clock-tower. "In half an hour," he said to himself, "he will bring it to her, aboard the yacht;" and he turned and re-entered the church. He went up the aisle, nodded to the sacristan, entered the treasury, took the turquoise cup, came out with it in his hand, nodded again to the sacristan, went down the steps, crossed the Piazza, ran down the landing-stairs, and jumped into a gondola.

"To the English yacht!" he cried.

He looked at his watch. "It seems," he said to himself "that one can join the criminal classes in about six minutes. I've twenty-four the start of Phelim."

They came alongside the Tara, and the earl sprang up the ladder.

"Lady Nora?" he asked of the quartermaster.

"She is below, my lord. She has just come aboard, and she left orders to show you down, my lord."

"Me?" exclaimed the earl.

"She didn't name you, my lord;" said the quartermaster, "what she said was—'A gentleman will come on board soon; show him below.'"

The earl speculated a moment as to whether he were still a gentleman, and then went down the companion-way. He came to the saloon. The door was open. He looked in. Lady Nora was seated at the piano, but her hands were clasped in her lap. Her head was bent and the earl noticed, for the thousandth time, how the hair clustered in her neck and framed the little, close-set ear. He saw the pure outlines of her shoulders; beneath the bench, he saw her foot in its white shoe; he saw, or felt, he could not have told you which, that here was the one woman in all this great world. To love her was a distinction. To sin for her was a dispensation. To achieve her was a coronation.

He tapped on the door. The girl did not turn, but she put her hands on the keys quickly, as if ashamed to have them found idle.

"Ah, Phelim," she said, "you are more than prompt; you never keep one waiting," and she began to play very softly.

The earl was embarrassed. Despite his crime, he still had breeding left him, and he felt compelled to make his presence known. He knocked again.

"Don't interrupt me, Phelim," she said; "this is my swan-song; listen;" and she began to sing. She sang bravely, at first, with her head held high, and then, suddenly, her voice began to falter.

"Ah, Phelim, dear," she cried, "I've lost my love! I've lost my love!" and she put her hands to her face and fell to sobbing.

"Nora!" said the earl. It was the first word he had spoken, and she raised her head, startled.

"Here is the cup, Nora," he said.

She sprang to her feet and turned to him, tears on her cheeks, but a light in her eyes such as he had never seen.

"Oh, my love," she cried, "I should have known you'd bring it."

"Yes," he said, "you should have known."

She stood, blushing, radiant, eager, waiting.

He stood in the doorway, pale, quiet, his arms at his side, the cup in his hand.

"Nora," he said, "I've brought you the cup, but I do not dare to give it to you. I stole it."

"What?" she cried, running toward him. She stopped suddenly and began to laugh—a pitiful little laugh, pitched in an unnatural key. "You shouldn't frighten me like that, Bobby," she said; "it isn't fair."

"It is true," said the earl; "I am a thief."

She looked at him and saw that he was speaking the truth.

"No," she cried, "'tis I am the thief, not you. The cardinal warned me that I was compelling you to this, and I laughed at him. I thought that you would achieve the cup, if you cared for me; that you would render some service to the State and claim it as your reward—that you would make a fortune, and buy it—that you would make friends at the Vatican—that you would build churches, found hospitals, that even the Holy Father might ask you to name something within his gift—I thought of a thousand schemes, such as one reads of—but I never thought you would take it. No, no; I never thought that."

"Nora," said the earl, "I didn't know how to do any of those things, and I didn't have time to learn."

"I would have waited for you, always," she said.

"I didn't know that," said the earl.

"I hoped you didn't," said Lady Nora. "Come!" and she sprang through the door. The earl followed her. They ran up the companion-way, across the deck, down the boarding-stairs. The earl's gondola was waiting.

"To the molo in five minutes," cried Lady Nora to the poppe, "and you shall be rich."

They went into the little cabin. The earl still held the cup in his hand. They sat far apart—each longing to comfort the other—each afraid to speak. Between them was a great gulf fixed—the gulf of sin and shame.

Half-way to the landing, they passed Phelim's gondola, making for the yacht. The cabin hid them and he passed in silence.

"I sent him for some bon-bons," said Lady Nora. "I did it to make you jealous."

They reached the molo in less than five minutes and Lady Nora tossed her purse to the oarsmen, and sprang out.

"Put the cup under your coat," she said. The earl obeyed. He had stolen it openly. He brought it back hidden. They crossed the Piazza as rapidly as they dared, and entered the church. The sacristan greeted them with a smile and led the way to the treasury.

"They haven't missed it yet," whispered Lady Nora.

The sacristan unlocked the outer and the inner door, bowed, and left them.

Lady Nora seized the cup and ran to its accustomed shelf. She had her hand outstretched to replace it, when she uttered a cry.

"What is it?" exclaimed the earl.

She did not answer, but she pointed, and the earl, looking where she pointed, saw, on the shelf—the turquoise cup.

They stared at the cup on the shelf—at the cup in Lady Nora's hand—and at each other—dumfounded.

They heard a limping step on the pavement and the cardinal came in. His face was very grave, but his voice was very gentle.

"My children," he said, "I prayed God that you would bring back the cup, but, *mea culpa*, I lacked faith, and dared not risk the original. Would God let Nora Blake's granddaughter make shipwreck? The cup you have, my child, is but silver-gilt and glass, but it may serve, some other day, to remind you of this day. Look at it when your pride struggles with your heart. Perhaps the sight of it may strengthen you. Take it, not as the present of a cardinal, or an archbishop, but as the wedding-gift of an old man who once was young, and once knew Nora Blake."

"A wedding-gift?" exclaimed Lady Nora. "What man would ever marry such a wretch as I?"

"Nora!" cried the earl; and he held out his arms.

"My pigeons are waiting for me," said the cardinal; and he went away, limping.

THE DESERT

Far down in the Desert of Sahara is the little oasis of El Merb. It is so small that our crude atlases miss it. It has but one well, and the fertile land is not more than forty rods in diameter. It has a mosque, a bazaar, a slave-market, and a café. It is called by the traders of Biskra "The Key of the Desert." It is called by the Mohammedan priests of Biskra "The Treasury of the Desert." It is called by the French commandant at Biskra "A place to be watched." The only communication between El Merb and Biskra is by camels, and Abdullah was once the chief caravan-master.

* * * * *

Abdullah, having felt the humps of his camels, turned to his driver.

"We start to-morrow, Ali," he said; "the beasts are fit."

Ali bowed and showed his white teeth.

"To-morrow," continued Abdullah, "since it is Friday; and immediately after the middle prayer. I hear in the bazaar that the well at Okba is choked. Can we make forty-two miles in one day, so as to cut Okba out?"

"We can," said Ali, "during the first three days, when the beasts do not drink; after that—no."

"Good," said Abdullah; "I will make a route."

Some one plucked at his sleeve and he turned.

"Sir," said a man with a white beard and eager eyes, "I learn that you start for Biskra to-morrow."

"If Allah wills," said Abdullah.

"In crossing the desert," said the old man, "I am told there are many dangers."

"Friend," said Abdullah, "in sitting at home there are many dangers."

"True," said the old man; and, after an interval, he added, "I think I may trust you."

Abdullah shrugged his shoulders and rolled a cigarette.

"Would it please you," said the old man, "to take a passenger for Biskra?"

"At a price," replied Abdullah, striking a match.

"What is the price?" asked the old man.

"Do you pay in dates, hides, ivory, or gold-dust?"

"In dust," replied the old man.

Abdullah threw away his cigarette. "I will carry you to Biskra," said he, "for eight ounces, and will furnish you with dates. If you desire other food, you must provide it. You shall have water, if I do."

"It is not for myself that I seek passage," said the old man, "but for my daughter."

"In that event," said Abdullah, "the price will be nine ounces. Women cast responsibility upon me."

"And her maid-servant?" asked the old man.

"Eight ounces," replied Abdullah.

"It is all I have," said the old man, "but I will give it."

"If you have no more," said Abdullah, "Allah forbid that I should strip you. I will carry the two for sixteen ounces."

"Allah will make it up to you," said the old man. "If you will deign to accompany me to the bazaar, I will pay you immediately."

They went to the arcades about the square and entered the shop of Hassan, the money-changer.

The old man pulled at his girdle and produced, after many contortions, a purse of gazelle skin.

"Friend Hassan," he said, "I wish to pay to this, my son, sixteen ounces. Kindly weigh them for me."

Hassan produced his scales. They consisted of two metal disks, suspended by silk threads from the ends of a fern stem. He balanced this stem upon the edge of a knife, fixed above his table. In one of the pans he placed a weight, stamped with Arabic characters. The pan fell to the table. Hassan produced a horn spoon, which he blew upon and then carefully wiped with the hem of his burnoose. He handed the spoon to the old man, who felt of the bowl.

"It is dry," he said; "nothing will stick to it."

Hassan plunged the spoon into the bag and brought it out, filled with gold-dust, which he poured into the empty pan. The scales rose, fell, trembled, and then settled even.

"I nearly always can judge an ounce," said Hassan; "a grain is another matter."

He weighed out sixteen ounces. The last ounce he left in the pan. Then he turned and, with a sweep of his arm, caught a fly from off the wall. He handled it with the greatest care until he held it in the tips of his fingers; then he put it into his mouth and closed his lips. In a moment he took it out. The fly was moist and dejected. He placed it upon the gold-dust in the pan. The fly began to beat its wings and work its legs. In a moment its color changed from blue-black to yellow. It was coated with gold-dust. Hassan lifted it with a pair of tweezers, and popped it into an inlaid box.

"My commission," he said. "Good-by. Allah be with you."

The old man tied up his bag, which seemed to be as heavy as ever.

"I thought," said Abdullah, glancing at the purse, "that seventeen ounces was all you had."

"What remains," said the old man, and there was a twinkle in his eye, "belongs to Allah's poor, of whom I am one."

"I regret," said Abdullah, with some heat, "that I did not treble my usual price. I merely doubled it for you."

The old man's face clouded, but only for an instant.

"My son," he said, "I am glad that I have intrusted my daughter to you. You will bring her to Biskra in safety. At what hour do you start?"

"Immediately after the noon prayer," answered Abdullah, "and I wait for no one."

"Good," said the old man, "we shall be there; *slama*."

"*Slama*," said Abdullah, and they parted.

Abdullah went back to his camels. He found Ali asleep between the black racer and the dun leader. He kicked him gently, as though he were a dog, and Ali sat up smiling and pleased to be kicked, when he saw his master.

"We take two women with us," said Abdullah.

"Allah help us," said Ali.

"He has already," said Abdullah; "I have sixteen ounces in my girdle."

"It seems, then," said Ali, grinning, "that not only Allah has helped you, but you have helped yourself."

"Peace," said Abdullah, "you know nothing of commerce."

"I know, however," said Ali, "that the Englishwoman whom we carried two years ago, and who made us stop two days at the wells of Okba, because her dog was ailing, gave me a bad piece of silver that I could not spend in Biskra. 'T was she of the prominent teeth and the big feet. I used to see her feet when she mounted her camel, and I used to see her teeth when I saw nothing else."

"Peace," said Abdullah. "Allah who made us made also the English."

"Perhaps," said Ali, "but one cannot help wondering why He did it."

"If we carry these two women," said Abdullah, "we must leave the cargo of two beasts behind. Leave four bales of hides; I took them conditioned upon no better freight offering; and put the women on the two lame camels. In this way we profit most, since we sacrifice least merchandise. The porters will be here at sunrise to help you load. See that they are careful. You remember what happened last time, when our cargoes kept shifting. All seems well tonight, except you have loaded that red camel yonder too high on the right side. How can a camel rest if, when he kneels, his load does not touch the ground? He must support the weight himself."

"I intended to alter that in the morning," said Ali.

"The morning may never dawn," said Abdullah, "and meanwhile you rob the beast of one night's rest. Attend to it at once. The speed of a caravan is the speed of its slowest camel."

"Who should know that better than I?" exclaimed Ali. "Have I not crossed the desert nine times with you? Oh, master, bear with me, I am growing old."

"What is your age?" asked Abdullah.

"One-and-thirty," replied Ali.

"My friend," said Abdullah, "you are good for another voyage; and know this, when you fail me, I quit the desert, and turn householder, with a wife or two, and children, if Allah wills it. I myself am six-and-twenty. I have earned a rest. *Slama*." And he turned on his heel to go, but he turned again.

"Ali," he said, "who lives in the first house beyond the mosque, on the left— the house with the green lattices?"

"I do not know, my master," replied Ali, "but I shall tell you in the morning."

"Good," said Abdullah; "and there is a damsel who sits behind the lattice, and always wears a flower in her hair, a red flower, a flower like this," and he put his hand into the folds of his burnoose and brought out a faded, crumpled, red oleander. "Who is she?"

"Tomorrow," said Ali.

"Good," said Abdullah, and he went away.

"*Slama*" said Ali, and then he added, to himself, "There goes a masterful man, and a just one, but love has caught him."

And he hurriedly eased the red camel of her load.

II

The next morning the departing caravan had many visitors. The merchants from the arcades came to see that their ventures were properly loaded. They passed comments upon the camels as Englishmen and Americans do upon horses in the paddock or the show-ring. Some they criticised, some they praised, but they were of one mind as to their condition.

"Their humps are fat," they all agreed; and, as a camel draws upon his hump for food as he draws upon the sacs surrounding his stomach for water, the condition of the caravan was declared to be *mleh*, which is the Arabic equivalent for "fit."

Abdullah was a busy man. He signed manifests, received money, receipted for it, felt of surcingles, tightened them, swore at the boys who were teasing the camels, kicked Ali whenever he came within reach, and in every way played the *rôle* of the business man of the desert.

Suddenly, from the minaret of the mosque came the cry of the mueddin. The clamor of the market ceased and the Mussulmans fell upon their knees, facing the east and Mecca. The camels were already kneeling, but they were facing the north and Biskra.

While the faithful were praying, the unbelievers from the Soudan fell back and stood silent. A cry to God, no matter what god, silences the patter of the market-place. Abdullah prayed as a child beseeches his father.

"Give me, Allah, a safe and quick journey. Unchoke the wells at Okba. Strengthen the yellow camel. Make high the price of dates and low the price of hides; 'tis thus I have ventured. Bring us in safety to Biskra. And bring me to the damsel who sits behind the green lattice. These things I pray—thy sinful son, Abdullah."

He rose, and the old man stood at his elbow. Abdullah had forgotten his passengers.

"This," said the old man, turning to a woman veiled to her eyes, "is my daughter, and this," he added, "is her maid," and a negress, comely and smiling, made salaam. "I pray thee," he continued, "to deliver this invoice," and he handed Abdullah a paper.

Abdullah was too busy to notice his passengers. "Let them mount at once," he said, slipping the paper under his girdle, and he left them to Ali, who came up showing his white teeth.

There were the last words, instructions, cautions, adieus, and then Abdullah held up his hand. Ali gave the cry of the camel-driver and the uncouth beasts, twisting and snarling under their loads, struggled to their feet.

Another cry, and they began their voyage. They traversed the square, passed the mosque, turned down a narrow street, and in five minutes crossed the line that bounded the oasis, and entered upon the desert.

Immediately the dun leader took his place at the left and slightly in advance. The fourth on the right of the dun was the black racer. He carried two water-skins and Abdullah's saddle. Then came, in ranks, fifteen camels, Ali riding in the centre. On the right flank rode the two women, with enormous red and white cotton sunshades stretched behind them. Then, at an interval of six rods, came fifteen camels unattended. They simply followed the squad in front. The dun leader and the black racer had lanyards about their necks. The other camels had no harness save the surcingles that held their loads.

In a panic, a sand-storm, a fusillade from Bedouins, a mirage, and a race for water, if Abdullah and Ali could grasp these lanyards, the caravan was saved, since the other camels followed the dun leader and the black racer as sheep follow the bell-wether.

Abdullah walked at the left, abreast of the dun. At intervals he rode the black racer.

The pace of a caravan is two miles an hour, but Abdullah's, the two cripples included, could make two miles and a quarter. The black racer could make sixty miles a day for five days, without drinking, but at the end of such a journey his hump would be no larger than a pincushion, and his temper—?

For centuries it has been the custom of Sahara caravans to travel not more than five miles the first day. Abdullah, the iconoclast, made thirty-three. Ali came to him at two o'clock.

"Shall we camp, master?" he asked.

"When I give the word," replied Abdullah. "You forget that the wells at Okba are choked. We shall camp at El Zarb."

"El Zarb," exclaimed Ali. "We should camp there to-morrow."

"Must I continually remind you," said Abdullah, "that to-morrow may never dawn? We camp at El Zarb to-night."

At nine o'clock they marched under the palms of El Zarb. Abdullah held up his hands; Ali ran to the head of the dun leader; the caravan halted, groaned, and knelt. The first day's journey was over.

III

The moment that the halt was accomplished, Abdullah went about, loosing the surcingles of his camels. Then he began to pitch his tent. It was of camel-skins, stretched over eight sticks, and fastened at the edges with spikes of locust wood. It was entirely open at the front, and when he had the flaps pinned, he gathered a little pile of camels' dung, struck a match, and began to make his tea. He had no thought for his passengers. His thoughts were with his heart, and that was back at the house beyond the bazaar—the house with the green lattices. Before the water boiled, Ali came up, eager, breathless.

"Master," he said, "the passengers are cared for, and the mistress wears a flower like—like *that*; the one you showed me;" and he pointed to Abdullah's bosom. "You are either a faithful servant," said Abdullah, "or you are a great liar. The morrow will tell." And he started toward the passengers' tent. He found it closed. Being a woman's tent, it had front flaps, and they were laced. He walked back and forth before it. He was master of the caravan, more autocratic than the master of a ship. He might have cut the laces, entered, and no one could have questioned. That is the law of the desert. He could more easily have cut his own throat than that slender cord.

He wandered back and forth before the tent. The twilight faded. The shadows turned from saffron to violet, to purple, to cobalt. Out of the secret cavern of the winds came the cool night-breeze of the Sahara.

Still he paced up and down, before the little tent. And as he measured the sands, he measured his life. Born of a camel-driver by a slave; working his way across the desert a score of times before his wages made enough to buy one bale of hides; venturing the earnings of a lifetime on one voyage—making a profit, when a loss would have put him back to the beginning—venturing again, winning again—buying three camels—leasing them—buying three more—starting an express from the Soudan to Biskra one day short of all others;—carrying only dates and gold-dust—insuring his gold-dust, something he learned from the French in Biskra;—buying thirty camels at a plunge—at once the master camel-driver of the Sahara—and here he was, pacing up and down before a laced tent which held behind it—*a woman.*

The night of the desert settled down, and still he paced. The stars came up—the stars by which he laid his course; and, finally, pacing, he came for the hundredth time to the tent's front and stopped.

"Mistress?" he whispered. There was no answer, "Mistress?" he called, and then, after an interval, the flies of the tent parted—a white hand, and a whiter wrist, appeared, and a red oleander fell on the sands of the desert.

Abdullah was on his knees. He pressed the flower to his lips, to his heart. Kneeling he watched the flaps of the tent. They fluttered; the laces raced through the eyelets; the flaps parted, and a girl, unveiled, stepped out into the firelight. They stood, silent, gazing one at the other.

"You have been long in coming," she said, at length.

There is no love-making in the desert. Thanks to its fervent heat, love there comes ready-made.

"Yes," said Abdullah, "I have tarried, but now that I have come, I stay forever;" and he took her in his arms.

"When did you love me first?" she whispered, half-released.

"When first I saw you, behind the green lattice," gasped Abdullah.

"Ah, that green lattice," whispered the girl; "how small its openings were. And still, my heart flew through them when first you passed. How proudly you walked. Walk for me now—here, in the firelight, where I may see you—not so slowly with your eyes turned toward me, but swiftly, smoothly, proudly, your head held high—that's it—that is the way you passed my lattice, and as you passed my heart cried out, 'There goes my king.' Did you not hear it?"

"No," said Abdullah; "my own heart cried so loudly I heard naught else."

"What did it cry? What cries it now?" she said; and she placed her cheek against his bosom, her ear above his heart. "I hear it," she whispered, "but it beats so fast I cannot understand."

"Then," said Abdullah, "I must tell thee with my lips."

"Oh, beloved," she whispered, "the camels will see us."

"What matters," he said; "they belong to me."

"Then they are my brethren," she said, "since I, also, belong to thee," and with arms entwined they passed out of the fire-light into the purple of the desert.

* * * * *

When they came back, the hobbled camels were snoring, and the unfed fires were smouldering.

"Allah keep thee," said Abdullah, at the door of her tent.

"And thee, my master," said the girl, and the flaps fell.

Abdullah went slowly toward his own tent. He stopped a moment by one of the lame camels. "Thou broughtest her to me," he said, and he eased the beast's surcingle by a dozen holes.

He reached his tent, paused, faced the western horizon, lifted his arms, breathed in the sweet, cool air of the desert, and entered.

Ali had spread a camel's hide, had covered a water-skin with a burnoose for a pillow, and had left, near it, a coiled wax-taper and a box of matches. Abdullah untwined his turban, loosened his sash, felt something escape him, fell on his knees, groped, felt a paper, rose, went to the tent's door, recognized the invoice which the old man had given him, went out, kicked up the embers of the fire, knelt, saw that the paper was unsealed, was fastened merely with a thread, played with the thread, saw it part beneath his fingers, saw the page unfold, stirred up the embers, and read:

"_To Mirza, Mother of the Dancers at Biskra, by the hand of Abdullah. I send thee, as I said, the most beautiful woman in the world. She has been carefully reared. She has no thought of commercialism. Two and two are five to her as well as four. She is unspoiled. She never has had a coin in her fingers, and she never has had a wish ungratified. She knows a little French; the French of courtship merely. Her Arabic is that of Medina. You, doubtless, will exploit her in Biskra. You may have her for two years. By that time she may toss her own handkerchief. Then she reverts to me. I shall take her to Cairo, where second-rate Englishmen and first-rate Americans abound.

"This is thy receipt for the thirty ounces you sent me._

"ILDERHIM."

When Abdullah had read this invoice of his love, he sat long before the little fire as one dead. Then he rose, felt in his bosom, and drew out two flowers, one withered, the other fresh. He dropped these among the embers, straightened himself; lifted his arms toward heaven, and slowly entered his tent.

The little fires smouldered and died, and the great desert was silent, save for the sighing of the camels and the singing of the shifting sands.

THE MAN WHO KEEPS GOATS

I

The next morning broke as all mornings break in the desert, first yellow, then white, and always silent. The air bore the scent of sage. The hobbled camels had broken every shrub within their reach, and stunted herbage is, almost always, aromatic.

Abdullah gave no heed to the sun. He who for ten years had been the most energetic man of the desert had overnight become the most nonchalant. Like Achilles, he sulked in his tent.

At five o'clock Ali ventured to bring his master's coffee. He found Abdullah fully dressed and reading a paper, which he hurriedly thrust into his burnoose when he was interrupted.

"Your coffee, master," said Ali. "We have twelve leagues to make to-day."

"Ali," said Abdullah, "the night before we started I asked you who lived in the house with the green lattices—the next house beyond the mosque—and you promised to tell me in the morning."

"Yes, master," said Ali, "but in the morning you did not ask me."

"I ask you now," said Abdullah.

Ali bowed. "Master," he answered, "the house is occupied by Ilderhim, chief of the tribe of Ouled Nail. He hires it for five years, and he occupies it for the three months, Chaban, Ramadan, and Chaoual, of each year. He has also the gardens and four water-rights. He deals in ivory, gold-dust, and dancing-girls. He formerly lived in Biskra, but the French banished him. They have also banished him from Algiers, and he has been warned from Cairo and Medina. He has a divorced wife in each of those cities. They are the mothers of the dancing-girls. The one in Biskra is Mirza. Every one in Biskra knows Mirza. Doubtless you, master—"

"Yes," said Abdullah, "but the damsel. Who is she?"

"His daughter," replied Ali.

"How know you this?" demanded Abdullah, fiercely.

"Master," said Ali, "last night, when you were looking at the stars with the mistress, I had a word with the maid. She came to me, while I was asleep by the dun leader, and shook me as if I had been an old friend.

"'Save her,' she whispered, as I rubbed my eyes.

"'Willingly,' I replied. 'Who is she?'

"'My mistress,' said the maid. 'They are taking her to Biskra. She has been sold to Mirza. She will dance in the cafés. This sweet flower will be cast into the mire of the market-place. Save her.'

"'How know you this?' I asked.

"'Ah,' she answered, 'this is not the first time I have crossed the desert with one of Ilderhim's daughters. Save her.'

"'Does the damsel know nothing of this—does she not go with her eyes open?' I asked.

"'She thinks,' said the maid, 'that she goes to Biskra to be taught the manners and the learning of the French women—to read, to sing, to know the world. Her heart is even fairer than her face. She knows no evil. Save her.'"

Abdullah groaned and hung his head.

"Forgive me, Allah," he said, "for that I doubted her. Forgive me for that I burned the flowers she gave to me," and he went out.

"Your coffee, master," cried Ali, but Abdullah paid no heed. He went swiftly to the little tent, and there was the damsel, veiled, and already mounted on the lame camel, ready to march.

"Beloved," said Abdullah, "you must dismount," and he lifted her from the back of the kneeling beast.

"Ali," he cried, "place the damsel's saddle on the black racer, and put mine on the dun. We two start on at once for the oasis of Zama. We can make it in thirteen hours. Give us a small water-skin and some dates. I leave everything else with you. Load, and follow us. We will wait for you at Zama. I go to counsel with the Man who Keeps Goats."

In five minutes the black racer and the dun leader were saddled.

"Come, beloved," said Abdullah, and without a word she followed him. She had asked no question, exhibited no curiosity. It was enough for her that Abdullah said, "Come."

They rode in silence for some minutes. Then Abdullah said: "Beloved, I do not know your name."

She dropped her veil, and his heart fell to fluttering.

"The one who loves me calls me 'beloved,'" she said, "and I like that name."

"But your real name?" said Abdullah.

"I was baptized 'Fathma,'" she said, smiling.

"Doubtless," said Abdullah; "since all women are named for the mother of the Prophet; but what is your other name, your house name?"

"Nicha," she answered; "do you like it?"

"Yes," he said, "I like it."

"I like 'beloved' better," said the girl.

"You shall hear it to your heart's content," said Abdullah.

They went on again, in silence, which was broken by the girl.

"Master," she said, "if you do not care to speak to me further, I will put up my veil."

"Do not," exclaimed Abdullah, "unless," he added, "you fear for your complexion."

"I do not fear for my complexion," said the girl, "but for my reputation; and she smiled again.

"That," said Abdullah, "is henceforth in my keeping. Pay no heed to it."

"I am not yet your wife," said the girl.

"True," said Abdullah, "and we are making this forced march to learn how I may make you such. Who is your father, beloved?"

"Ilderhim," she answered; "but why do you ask? You saw him when we started from El Merb."

"Do you love him?" asked Abdullah.

"I scarcely know," answered the girl, after a pause. "I have not seen him often. He is constantly from home. He buys me pretty clothes and permits me to go to the cemetery each Friday with my maid. I suppose I love him—not as I love you, or as I love the camel that brought me to you, or the sandal on your foot, or the sand it presses—still, I think I must love him—but I never thought about it before."

"And your mother?" asked Abdullah.

"I have no mother," said the girl. "She died before I can remember."

"And why do you go to Biskra?" asked Abdullah.

"My father sends me," said the girl, "to a great lady who lives there. Her name is Mirza. Do you not know her, since you lived in Biskra?"

Abdullah did not answer. Something suddenly went wrong with his saddle, and he busied himself with it.

"I am to be taught the languages and the ways of Europe," continued the girl, "music and dancing, and many things the desert cannot teach. I am to remain two years, and then my father fetches me. Now that I consider the trouble and expense he is put to on my account, surely I should love him, should I not?"

Abdullah's saddle again required attention.

They rode for hours, sometimes speaking, sometimes silent. Twice Abdullah passed dates and water to the girl, and always they pressed on. A camel does not trot, he paces. He moves the feet of his right side forward at once, and follows them with the feet of his left side. This motion heaves the rider wofully. The girl stood it bravely for six hours, then she began to droop. Abdullah watched her as her head sank toward the camel's neck; conversation had long ceased. It had become a trial of endurance. Abdullah kept his eye upon the girl. He saw her head bending, bending toward her camel's neck; he gave the cry of halt, leaped from the dun, while yet at speed, raced to the black, held up his arms and caught his mistress as she fell.

There was naught about them save the two panting camels, the brown sands, the blue sky, and the God of Love. Abdullah lifted her to the earth as tenderly, as modestly, as though she had been his sister. It is a fine thing to be a gentleman, and the God of Love is a great God.

It proved that the girl's faintness came from the camel's motion and the cruel sun. Abdullah made the racer and the dun kneel close together. He spread his burnoose over them and picketed it with his riding-stick. This made shade. Then he brought water from the little skin; touched the girl's lips with it, bathed her brow, sat by her, silent, saw her sleep; knelt in the sand and kissed the little hand that rested on it, and prayed to Him that some call God, and more call Allah.

In an hour the girl whispered, "Abdullah?"

He was at her lips.

"Why are we waiting?" she asked.

"Because I was tired," he answered.

"Are you rested?" she asked.

"Yes," he answered.

"Then let us go on," she said.

They rode on, hope sustaining Abdullah, and love sustaining Nicha, for she knew nothing but love.

Then, after eight hours, on the edge of the desert appeared a little cloud, no larger than a man's hand.

Abdullah roused himself with effort. He watched the cloud resolve itself into a mass of green, into waving palms—then he knew that Zama was before him, and that the march was ended.

He turned and spoke to the girl. They had not spoken for hours. "Beloved," he said, "a half-hour, and we reach rest."

She did not answer. She was asleep upon her saddle.

"Thank Allah," said Abdullah, and they rode on.

Suddenly the trees of the oasis were blotted out. A yellow cloud of dust rolled in between them and the travellers, and Abdullah said to himself, "It is he whom I seek—it is He who Keeps Goats."

II

They met. In the midst of threescore goats whose feet had made the yellow cloud of dust was a man, tall, gaunt, dressed in the garb of the desert, and burned by the sun as black as a Soudanese.

"Ah, my son," he cried, in French, when he was within distance, "you travel light this time. Whom have you with you, another mistress, or, at last, a wife?"

"Hush," said Abdullah, "she is a little damsel who has ridden twelve leagues and is cruel tired."

"God help her," said the man of the goats; "shall I give her some warm milk—there is plenty?"

"No," said Abdullah; "let us go to thy house," and the goats, at the whistle of their master, turned, and followed the camels under the palms of the oasis of Zama.

They halted before a little hut, and Abdullah held up his hand. The camels stopped and kneeled. The girl did not move. Abdullah ran to her, took her in his arms, lifted her, turned, entered the hut, passed to the inner room, laid her upon a low couch, beneath the window, put away her veil, kissed her hand, not her lips, and came out.

In the outer room he found his host. Upon the table were some small cheeses, a loaf of bread, a gourd of milk. Abdullah fell upon the food.

"Well, my son," said his host, after Abdullah began to pick and choose, "what brings you to me?"

"This," said Abdullah, and he felt in his bosom, and drew out the invoice of his passenger.

His host took from a book upon the table a pair of steel-bowed spectacles—the only pair in the Sahara. He placed the bow upon his nose, the curves behind his ears, snuffed the taper with his fingers, took the invoice from Abdullah, and read. He read it once, looked up, and said nothing. He read it a second time, looked up, and said: "Well, what of it?"

"Is it legal?" asked Abdullah.

"Doubtless," said his host, "since it is a hiring, merely, not a sale; and it is to be executed in Biskra, which is under the French rule."

"The French rule is beneficent, doubtless?" asked Abdullah.

His host did not answer for some minutes; then he said: "It is a compromise; and certain souls deem compromises to be justice. The real men of this age, as of all others, do not compromise; they fight out right and wrong to a decision. The French came into Algeria to avenge a wrong. They fought, they conquered, and then they compromised. Having compromised, they must fight and conquer all over again."

"You are a Frenchman, are you not?" asked Abdullah.

"No," replied his host, "I am a Parisian."

"Ah," exclaimed Abdullah, "I thought they were the same thing."

"Far from it," replied his host. "In Brittany, Frenchmen wear black to this day for the king whom Parisians guillotined."

"Pardon," said Abdullah; "I have been taught that Paris is French."

"Not so, my son," rejoined his host; "Paris is universal. If you will go to the Museum of the Louvre, and take a seat before the Venus of Milo, and will remain long enough, everybody in this world, worth knowing, will pass by you; crowned heads, diplomats, financiers, the demimonde; you may meet them all. They tell me that the same thing happens to the occupant of the corner table of the Café de la Paix—the table next to the Avenue de l'Opéra; if he waits long enough, he will see every one—"

"Pardon me, Monsieur," said Abdullah, "but I care to see no one save the little maid sleeping within."

"Ah," said his host, "it is love, is it? I thought it was commercialism."

"No," said Abdullah; "it is a question of how I can keep the woman I love, and still keep my commercial integrity. She is consigned to me by her father, to be delivered to Mirza, the mother of the dancers, in Biskra. I am the trusted caravan owner between El Merb and Biskra. In the last ten years I have killed many men who tried to rob my freight of dates, and hides, and gold-dust. Now I long to rob my own freight of the most precious thing I have ever carried. May I do it, and still be a man; or must I deliver the damsel, re-cross the desert, return the passage money to her father, come once more to Biskra, and find my love the sport of the cafés?"

The Man who Keeps Goats rose and paced the floor.

"My son," he said, finally, "when the French occupied Algeria, they made this bargain—'Mussulmans shall be judged by their civil law.' It was a compromise and, therefore, a weakness. The civil law of the Mohammedans is, virtually, the Koran. The law of France is, virtually, the Code Napoléon. The parties to the present contract being Mohammedans, it will be construed by their law, and it is not repugnant to it. If, on the contrary, the damsel were a Christian, the French commandant at Biskra would tear the contract to pieces, since it is against morals. Better yet, if *you* were a Christian, and the damsel your wife, you might hold her in Biskra against the world."

Abdullah sat silent, his eyes half closed.

"Monsieur," he said at length, "is it very difficult to become a Christian?"

The Man who Keeps Goats sat silent—in his turn.

"My son," he said, finally, "I myself am a priest of the Church. I have lived in the desert for twenty years, but I have never been unfrocked. I cannot answer you, but I can tell you what a wiser than I declared to a desert traveller who put this same question nineteen hundred years ago."

He took up the book upon the table, turned a few pages, and read—"'And the angel of the Lord spake unto Philip, saying, Arise, and go toward the south unto the way that goeth down from Jerusalem unto Gaza, which is desert. And he arose and went: and, behold, a man of Ethiopia, a eunuch of great authority under Candace queen of the Ethiopians, who had the charge of all her treasure, and had come to Jerusalem for to worship, was returning, and sitting in his chariot read Esaias the prophet…. And Philip ran thither to *him*, and heard him read the prophet Esaias, and said, Understandest thou what thou readest? And he said, How can I, except some man should guide me? And he desired Philip that he would come up and sit with him…. Then Philip opened his mouth, and began at the same scripture, and preached unto him Jesus. And as they went on *their* way, they came unto a certain water: and the eunuch said, See, *here is* water; what doth hinder me to be baptized?

"'And Philip said, If thou believest with all thine heart, thou mayest. And he answered and said, I believe that Jesus Christ is the Son of God.

"'And he commanded the chariot to stand still: and they went down both into the water, both Philip and the eunuch; and he baptized him.'"

Scarcely had the reader ceased when Abdullah sprang to his feet. "Father," he cried, "see, *here* is water. What doth hinder *me* to be baptized?"

"My son," said the old man, "how canst thou believe with all thine heart? No Philip has preached Jesus unto thee."

"What need?" exclaimed Abdullah. "Can a man's belief need preaching to in such a case as this? How long must I believe a religion that saves her I love? A month, a year, until it avails nothing, and she is gone? This eunuch was a blacker man than I; like me, he was a man of the desert. He did not ride with Philip long. I have not only heard what Philip said to him, but I have also heard what you have said to me. Both of you have preached unto me Jesus. What right have you to doubt my belief in a God who will save my love to me? Again, I ask you, what doth hinder me to be baptized?"

"Nothing," said the old man, and they went out both to the well, sparkling beneath the palms, both Abdullah and the Man who Keeps Goats; and he baptized him.

When Abdullah rose from his knees, his forehead dripping, he drew his hand across his face and asked, "Am I a Christian?"

"Yes," said the priest, "so far as I can make you one."

"Thank you," said Abdullah; "you have done much, and in the morning you shall do more, for then you shall baptize the damsel and shall marry us according to your—pardon me—our religion."

They entered the hut, and the priest, pointing toward the chamber-door, asked: "Does she believe?"

"She believes what I believe," said Abdullah.

The priest shook his head. "You speak," he said, "not as a Christian, but as a Moslem. You were brought up to look upon woman as a mere adjunct, a necessary evil, necessary because men must be born into the world. A female child, with you, was a reproach; she was scarcely seen by her parents until she was brought out to be sold in marriage. With Christians it is different. A woman has a soul—"

"Hush," said Abdullah, "or you will awaken the camels with that strange doctrine. A woman has a soul, has she? You read me no such proposition from your prophets, a half-hour ago. Woman was not mentioned by Philip or by the Ethiopian in what you read to me. Is there aught in your book that argues that woman has a soul?"

"Doubtless," said the priest, "but I do not recall it."

He caught up his Bible. He opened it unluckily, for the first words that met his eye were these, and he read them: "Woman, what have I to do with thee?" and he paused, embarrassed.

"Whose words were those?" asked Abdullah.

The priest hesitated, crossed himself, and answered: "They were the words of Jesus."

"To whom were they spoken?" asked Abdullah.

The answer lagged. Finally, the priest said, "To His mother."

"Master," said Abdullah, "the more I learn of my new religion, the more I am enamoured of it;" and he went to the chamber-door and knocked.

"Beloved," he said, and waited.

He knocked again, and again he said, "Beloved."

"Who art thou?" came a voice.

"'Tis I, Abdullah," he said.

"Enter," said the voice.

"Not so," said Abdullah; "but come you out."

"Art thou alone?" asked the voice.

"No," replied Abdullah, "the man who keeps goats is here."

"I have no light," said the voice.

Abdullah took the taper from the table, opened the door six inches, felt a warm soft hand meet his own, pressed it, left the taper in it, closed the door, and groped in darkness to his seat.

"Father," he said, after some moments of silence, "*have* women souls?"

"Doubtless," answered the priest.

"God help them," said Abdullah; "have they not trouble enough, without souls to save?"

The two men sat silent in the darkness.

The door creaked, a line of light appeared; the door swung wide out, and on the threshold stood Nicha, the taper in her hand.

The two men sat silent, gazing.

She had put off her outer costume of white linen and stood dressed for the house, the seraglio. Upon her head was a *chachia*, a little velvet cap, embroidered with seed-pearls. Her bust was clothed with a *rlila*, or bolero of brocaded silk, beneath which was a vest of muslin, heavy with gold buttons. About her slim waist was a *fouta*, or scarf of striped silk. Below came the *serroual*, wide trousers of white silk that ended mid-leg. Upon her feet were blue velvet slippers, pointed, turned up at the toes and embroidered with gold. About her ankles were *redeefs*, or bangles of emeralds, pierced, and strung on common string. At her wrists hung a multitude of bangles, and on her bare left arm, near the shoulder, was a gold wire that pinched the flesh, and from it hung a filigree medallion that covered her crest, tattooed beneath the skin. It is always so with the tribe of Ouled Nail.

This was the costume of the woman, but the woman herself, as she stood in the doorway, the taper in her hand, who may describe her? Tall, lithe, laughing—her black hair, braided, tied behind her neck, and still reaching the ground; her eyebrows straight as though pencilled; her ears small and closely set; her nose straight and thin, with fluttering nostrils; her shoulders sloping; her bust firm and pulsating beneath her linen vest; her slender waist; her little feet, in the blue velvet slippers; the charm of breeding and of youth; the added charm of jewels and of soft textures; what wonder that the two men sat silent and gazing?

Abdullah spoke first. "Beloved," he said, "I have broken your night's rest that you may have eternal rest."

The girl laughed. "That is a long way off," she said. "The cemetery, with the cypress-trees, is beautiful, but this hut, with thee, is better. Why did you wake me?"

"Because, since you slept," said Abdullah, "I have changed my religion."

"Good," exclaimed the girl; "then I change mine. I am tired of a religion that makes me plait my hair for eight hours of the day and sends no man to see it."

"What religion do you choose?" asked Abdullah.

"Yours," said the girl, seating herself and dropping her hands, interlaced, and covered with turquoise rings, about her knees; "why should a woman question anything when her husband has passed upon it?"

"Did I not tell thee?" said Abdullah.

"Yes," said the priest, "but I waited for her own words."

"You have them now," said Abdullah, and they went out to the spring.

"I name thee Marie," said the priest, "since it is the name borne by the Mother of our Lord."

"Ah," said the girl, "I was baptized Fathma, after the Mother of the Prophet. There seems to be not so much difference thus far."

When the sacrament had been administered and they had returned to the hut, the priest addressed his converts. "My children," he said, "in order to do a great right I have done a little wrong. I have baptized you into a religion that you know nothing of. How should you? You, Abdullah—I beg your pardon, Philip—that was the name I gave you, was it not?"

Abdullah bowed.

"You, Philip," resumed the priest, "have changed your religion to win a woman whom you love; and you, Marie, have changed yours because the man you love bade you. Neither of you knows anything of the faith you have adopted. I have had no chance to instruct you; but one thing I declare to you, the Christian religion tolerates but one husband and one wife."

Nicha rose, pale, hesitating. She stepped slowly into the light. Her beauty added to the light.

"Beloved," she said, "knew you this?"

"No," he said, "but I know it now, and welcome it."

"Oh, my beloved," she cried, "to think that you are all my own, that I do not have to share you," and she flung her arms about him.

"Hush," said the priest, "or, as Philip says, you will wake the camels."

"Father," asked Abdullah, "will you now marry us, since we are Christians?"

"I would," answered the priest, "but it is necessary to have two witnesses."

Abdullah's face fell, but in an instant it brightened again. He went to the door of the hut and stood, listening. In a moment he turned and said, "Allah is good, or, rather, God is good. This new religion works well. Here are our witnesses."

And, even as he spoke, there came out of the darkness the halt-cry of the camel-driver.

"It is Ali," said Abdullah, "and Nicha's maid is with him. They have caught us up."

He ran out and found the camels kneeling and Ali easing the surcingles.

"Ali," he cried, "you must change your religion."

"Willingly," said Ali; "what shall the new one be? The old one has done little for me."

"Christian," said Abdullah.

"That suits me," said Ali; "under it one may drink wine, and one may curse. It is a useful religion for a trader."

"And the maid?" asked Abdullah.

"We have travelled a day and a part of a night together," said Ali, "and she will believe what I tell her to believe."

"The old religion is good in some respects," said Abdullah. "Call the maid;" and they went to the hut.

"Here are the witnesses," said Abdullah, "ready to be Christians."

"It is not necessary," said the priest, "if they can make their mark; that is all that is required."

So, in the little hut, before an improvised altar, they were married—the camel-driver and the daughter of the Chief of Ouled Nail.

The next morning the caravan took up the march for Biskra.

THE MOTHER OF THE ALMEES

It was the great fast of Rhamadan, and the square of Biskra was crowded with white-robed men waiting for the sun to set that they might eat.

The rough pavement was dotted with fires over which simmered pots filled with what only a very jealous God indeed would have called food. About them were huddled the traders from the bazaars, the camel-drivers from the desert, the water-carriers from Bab el Derb. Each man held a cigarette in his left hand and a match in his right. He would smoke before he ate.

In the long arcades the camels, in from the Soudan, knelt, fasting. An Arab led a tame lion into the square and the beast held back on his chain as he passed the flesh-pots, for he, too, was fasting. Crowds of little children stood about the circle of the fires, fasting. A God was being placated by the sufferings of His creatures.

There is little twilight in the latitude of Biskra. There is the hard, white light of the daytime, five minutes of lavender and running shadows, and then the purple blackness of the night.

The mueddin took his place on the minaret of the mosque. His shadow ran to the centre of the square and stopped. He cried his admonition, each white-robed figure bowed to the earth in supplication, a cannon-shot at the citadel split the hot air, and in an instant the square was dotted with sparks. Each worshipper had struck his match. The fast was over until sunrise.

The silence became a Babel. All fell to eating and to talking. A marabout, graceful as a Greek statue, came out of the mosque and made his way among the fires. As he passed, the squatting Mussulmans caught at his robe and kissed it. Mirza, the mother of the Almee girls, her golden necklaces glinting in the firelight, came walking by. As she passed the marabout he drew back and held his white burnoose across his face. She bent her knee and then went on, but as she passed she laughed and whispered, "Which trade pays best, yours or mine?" and she shook her necklaces.

"Daughter," said the marabout, "there is but one God."

"Yes," she replied, "but He has many prophets, and, of them all, you are the most beautiful," and she went on.

An officer of *spahis* rode in and, stopping his horse before the arched door of the commandant, stood motionless. The square was filled with color, with life, with foreignness, with the dancing flames, the leaping shadows, the fumes of the cook-pots, the odor of Arabian tobacco, the clamor of all the dialects of North Africa.

A bugle sounded. Out of a side street trotted a cavalcade. The iron shoes of the horses rang on the pavement, and the steel chains of the curbs tinkled. The commandant dismounted and gave his bridle to his orderly.

The commandant walked through the square. He wore a fatigue cap, a sky-blue blouse, with white loopings, white breeches, tight at the knee, and patent-leather boots, with box spurs. He walked through the square slowly, smoking cigarette after cigarette. He was not only the commandant but he was the commissioner of police. With seventy men he ruled ten thousand, and he knew his weakness. The knowledge of his weakness was his strength.

As he walked through the square he met Mirza. He passed her without a sign of recognition and she, on her part, was looking at the minaret of the mosque.

In their official capacities they were strangers. On certain occasions, when the commandant was in *mufti* they had, at least, passed the time of day. The commandant walked through the long rows of fires, speaking to a merchant here, nodding to a date-grower there, casting quick glances and saying nothing to the spies who, mingling with the people, sat about the kouss-kouss pots, and reported to the commandant, each morning, the date set for his throat-cutting. This was many years ago, before there was a railroad to Biskra.

The commandant, having made the round of the fires, crossed over to his house under the arcades. He dismissed the sergeant and the guard, and they rode away to the barracks, the hoof-beats dying in the distance. The *spahi* remained, silent, motionless. The commandant was about to enter his door, when a man sprang from behind one of the pillars of the arcade and held out to him a paper. The commandant put his hands behind his back. The *spahi* edged his horse up closely.

"Who are you?" asked the commandant, in French.

The man shook his head, but still held out the paper.

"Who are you?" asked the commandant again, but now in Arabic.

"I am Ali, the slave of Abdullah," answered the man, "and he sends you this letter."

The commandant remained motionless. "Will your horse stand, corporal?" he asked of the *spahi*.

"Perfectly, my colonel."

"Leave him, then," said the commandant, "and bring one of your pistols."

The *spahi* gathered his long blue cloak off the quarters of his horse, took a revolver from its holster, swung his right leg over his horse's head, so that he might not for an instant turn his back, threw the reins over his horse's neck, brought the heels of his red boots together, saluted, and stood silent.

The horse began to play with the pendant reins and to shift his loosened bit.

"Go in," said the commandant, and the *spahi* opened the door. "You next," and Ali followed. The commandant brought up the rear.

They entered at once not a hall but a room. So all Eastern houses are ordered. A lamp was burning, the walls were hung with maps of France and of North Africa, a few shelves held a few books and many tin cases labelled "Forage," "Hospital," "Police." Behind a desk sat a little man, dressed in black, who was dealing cards to himself in a game of solitaire. He rose and bowed when the commandant entered, and then he went on with his game.

"Stand there," said the commandant, pointing to a corner, "and put your hands over your head."

Ali obeyed.

"Search him," said the commandant.

The *spahi* began at Ali's hair and ended with his sandals.

"He has nothing," he reported.

"Now give me the letter," said the commandant.

Ali twisted himself, fumbled at his waist, and drew out a knife. He placed it on the desk, smiling.

"Do not blame the corporal for overlooking this," he said; "I am so thin from the journey that he took it for one of my ribs."

"I will trust you," said the commandant, and he took the letter.

The little man in black kept dealing solitaire.

The commandant read the letter to himself and laughed, and then he read it aloud:

"*To Monsieur the COUNT D'APREMONT, Commandant at Biskra.

"MONSIEUR: Since last I saw you strange things have happened. I have turned Christian, and I have married. I wonder at which of these statements you will laugh most.

"May I bring my wife to your house? She will be the only Christian woman in Biskra. Say 'yes' or 'no' to the bearer. I am halted a mile outside of the town, awaiting your answer.

"Mirza, the mother of the Almees, has a certain claim upon my wife; how valid I do not know. I need counsel, but first of all I need shelter. May I come?_

"ABDULLAH."

"Of course he may come," said the commandant; "what is to prevent?"

"The law, perhaps," said the little man in black, shuffling the cards.

The commandant turned quickly. "Why the law, Monsieur the Chancellor?" he asked.

"Because," answered the little man, still shuffling the cards, "he says that Mirza has a certain claim upon his wife, how valid he does not know; and he needs counsel and he needs shelter. When a man writes like this, he also needs a lawyer;" and he commenced a new deal.

The commandant stood a moment, thinking. Then he raised his head with a jerk, and said to Ali: "Tell your master that I say 'yes.'"

Ali made salaam and glided from the room.

"He has left his knife," said the lawyer.

The commandant turned to the *spahi*. "Corporal," he said, "go to the citadel and bring back twelve men. Place six of them at the entrance of the square, and six of them before my house. When Abdullah's caravan has entered the square, have the further six close in behind. You may take your time. It will be an hour before you are needed."

The *spahi* saluted, and went out.

The commandant turned to the little man in black.

"Why in the world," he asked, "did you object to my harboring Abdullah? He is my friend and yours. He is the best man that crosses the desert. He has eaten our salt many times. If all here were like him, you and I might go home to France, with our medals and our pensions."

"True," said the lawyer, gathering his cards, "and very likely there is no risk in harboring him and his wife." He shuffled the cards mechanically, his eyes fixed on the opposite wall.

"My friend," he said, at length, "whom do you consider the most powerful person in Biskra, the person to be first reckoned with?"

The commandant laughed. "As I am in command," he said, "I should be court-martialled if I denied my own superiority."

"And yet," said the lawyer, "you are only a poor second."

The commandant, who was sitting astride of his chair, his hands upon its back, demi-vaulted as if he were in the saddle of a polo pony.

"What do you mean?" he demanded.

The lawyer kept shuffling the cards, but he paid no attention to them.

"Go to the window," he said, "and tell me what you see."

The commandant rose, and went to the window, his spurs jingling. He drew the curtain and looked out.

"What do you see?" asked the counsellor.

"I see the square," answered the commandant, "with five hundred kettle-lights, and three thousand Mussulmans gorging themselves, making up lost time."

"Look over at the left corner," said the lawyer.

"I see the mosque," said the commandant, "with its lamps burning."

"There you have it," cried the lawyer. "This religion that you and I are sent to conquer keeps its lamps burning constantly, while the religion that comes to conquer lights its candles only for the mass. Mankind loves light and warmth. What do you see now?"

"I see Mirza," replied the commandant; "she is walking up the centre line of the fires. Now she stops. She meets a man, draws him hurriedly aside, and is speaking close to his ear."

"Has he a green turban?" asked the lawyer. "Has he been to Mecca?"

"Yes," answered the commandant.

"There you see the most powerful person in Biskra," said the counsellor.

"Who?" asked the commandant. "The man in the green turban?"

"No," said the lawyer, "the woman he is speaking to."

"Mirza?" exclaimed the commandant.

"Yes," said the lawyer. "The centre of affairs, since the world was sent spinning, has always been a woman. Who placed the primal curse of labor on the race? Was it the man, Adam, or the woman, Eve?"

"As I remember," said the commandant, "the serpent was the prime mover in that affair."

"Yes," said the lawyer; "but being 'more subtile than any beast in the field,' he knew that if he caught the woman the man would follow of his own accord. Julius Caesar and Antony were dwarfed by Cleopatra. Helen of Troy set the world ablaze. Joan of Arc saved France. Catharine I saved Peter the Great. Catharine II made Russia. Marie Antoinette ruled Louis XVI and lost a crown and her head. Fat Anne of England and Sarah Jennings united England and Scotland. Eugénie and the milliners lost Alsace and Lorraine. Victoria made her country the mistress of the world. I have named many women who have played great parts in this drama which we call life. How many of them were good women? By 'good' I do not mean virtuous, but simply 'good.'"

"Out of your list," said the commandant, "I should name Joan of Arc and Victoria."

"A woman," repeated the lawyer, "is the centre of every affair. When you go back to France, what are you looking forward to?"

"My wife's kiss," said the commandant. "And you, since you are a bachelor?"

"The scolding of my housekeeper," said the lawyer, and he shrugged his shoulders.

The commandant laughed. "But what of Mirza?" he asked. "Why is she so powerful?"

"For the same reason that your wife and my housekeeper are powerful," said the lawyer; "she is a woman."

"A woman here," said the commandant, "is a slave."

"A *good* woman, I grant you," said the lawyer, "but a *bad* woman, if she chance to be beautiful, is an empress. Do you know how many men it takes to officer a mosque of the first class, such a one as we have here? Twelve," and he dropped the cards and began to count his fingers. "Two *mueddins* the chaps that call to prayer; two *tolbas* who read the litanies; two *hezzabin*, who read the Koran; a *mufti* who interprets the law; a *khetib* who recites the prayer for the chief of the government each Friday, and who is very unpopular; an *iman* who reads the five daily prayers; a *chaouch* who is a secretary to the last of the list, the *oukil* who collects the funds and pays them out. The *oukil* is the man who governs the mosque. He is the man in the green turban whom you saw talking with Mirza. They are partners. He attends to the world, she to the flesh, and both to the devil. It is a strong partnership. It is what, in America, they call a 'trust.' The *oukil* sends his clients to Mirza, and she sends hers to the *oukil*. Look out of the window again. There are three thousand religionists who have passed through the hands of the *oukil* and Mirza, and she, making the most money, has the last word. Do you ask, now, why she is the most powerful person in Biskra?"

"It seems," said the commandant, "that it is because she is a woman, and is bad."

"And beautiful," added the lawyer.

"Do you think her beautiful?" asked the commandant.

The lawyer thought a moment. "Did you ever see a hunting-leopard?" he asked.

"No," said the commandant.

"I used to see them," said the lawyer, "when I was in Sumatra, looking after the affairs of some Frenchmen who were buying pearls from the oyster-beds of Arippo. They were horribly beautiful. Mirza reminds me of them, especially when she seizes her prey. Most beasts of prey are satisfied when they have killed all that they can devour; but the hunting-leopard kills because she loves to kill. So does Mirza. She destroys because she loves to destroy. A hunting-leopard and Mirza are the only two absolutely cruel creatures I have ever seen. Of course," he added, "I eliminate the English, who deem the day misspent unless they have killed something, and who give infinite pains and tenderness to the raising of pheasants, that they may slaughter a record number of them at a *battue*. Aside from a hunting-leopard and a hunting-Englishman, I know of no being so cruel as Mirza; no being that takes such delight in mere extermination. They used to call our nobility, in the time of Louis XIV and Louis XV, cruel, but they did not kill, they merely taxed. In the height of the ancient *régime*, it was not good form to kill a peasant, because then the country had one less taxpayer. The height of the art was to take all the peasant had and then to induce him to set to work again. When he had earned another surplus, his lord came and took it. France had an accomplished nobility. England had a brutal one. The latter used to take all the eggs out of the nest and then kill the hen. The French noble took all the eggs but one or two, and spared the hen. He could rob a nest a dozen times and his English contemporary could rob it but once."

"My friend," said the commandant, laughing, "you reassure me. When you begin comparing England with France, I know that you have nothing of importance at hand and that your mind is kicking up its heels in vacation. You have a charming mind, my friend, but it has been prostituted to the law. If you had been bred a soldier—"

He stopped, because the murmur of the square suddenly stopped. The cessation of a familiar clamor is more startling than a sudden cry. The two men ran to the window. The fires under the pots were still burning and the square was light as day. At the opposite side, where the caravan road debouched, three thousand white-robed Mussulmans stood, silent. Above them the commandant and the lawyer could see the heads of the six *spahis*, they and their horses silent. Beyond, were the heads of many camels. The commandant threw up the sash. Across the silent square came a woman's voice, speaking Arabic in the dialect of Ouled Nail.

"That is Mirza," said the lawyer.

Then there came a man's voice, evidently in reply.

"That is Abdullah," said the lawyer.

"How can you distinguish at this distance?" asked the commandant.

The lawyer shrugged his shoulders. "While you are drilling your soldiers," he said, "I am drilling myself. If a man yonder sneezes, I can name his tribe. A sneeze, being involuntary, cannot be artificial, and therefore it is the true index of race and character. Take the Oriental Express any night from Paris to Vienna. If you will sit up late enough and walk up and down the aisle, you may tell from the sneezes and the coughs the nationality of the occupant of each berth. A German sneezes with all his might, and if there is a compatriot within hearing he says, '*Gesundheit.*' An Italian sneezes as if it were a crime, with his hand over his face."

"Hush," said the commandant.

Out from the white-robed crowd came two forms, Mirza and the *oukil*. Mirza held a paper in her hand. They went to the nearest fire and Mirza gave the paper to the man with the green turban. He read it, thought a moment, read it again, and then the two went back to the silent crowd by the mosque. There was conversation, there were vehement exclamations which, if they had been in English, would have been oaths—there was a sudden movement of the horses and the camels; the outskirts of the crowd surged and broke, and then, above their heads, flashed the sabres of the *spahis*.

The commandant went to the door. "Corporal," he said, "take your men to the mosque, join your comrades, and bring to me Abdullah, his wife, Mirza, and the *oukil*."

The corporal saluted, gave an order, and the little troop trotted across the square. The commandant closed the shutters of the window.

"I do not care to see the row," he said, and he lit a cigarette. But if he did not see the row, he heard it, for presently came the yelp and snarl of an Oriental mob.

"It is growing warm," said the commandant. "Hospitality cannot be lightly practised here."

"Nor anywhere," said the lawyer, who had resumed his cards; "because it is a virtue, and the virtues are out of vogue. The only really successful life, as the world looks upon success now, is an absolutely selfish life. It is the day of specialists, of men with one idea, one object, and the successful man is the one who permits nothing to come between him and his object. Wife, children, honor, friendship, ease, all must give place to the grand pursuit; be it the gathering of wealth, the discovery of a disease germ, the culture of orchids, or the breeding of a honey-bee that works night and day. Human life is too short to permit a man to do more than one thing well, and money is becoming so common that its possessors require the best of everything."

"Old friend," said the commandant, "you are a many-sided man, and yet you are one of the best lawyers in France."

"You have said it," exclaimed the lawyer; "*one* of the best, not *the* best. The one thing I have earnestly striven for I have not attained."

"What is that?" asked the commandant. "Do you wish to be Minister of Justice?"

"No," said the lawyer; "but I should like to be known as the best player of Napoleon solitaire."

A sabre-hilt rapped on the door.

"Enter," cried the commandant.

The door opened, and there entered first the sharp cries of the mob, and then the corporal, Abdullah, a woman clothed all in white, the *oukil*, and, last of all, Mirza. The moment she was within the room she dominated it. The other occupants were blotted out by comparison. She entered, debonair, smiling, and, as she crossed the threshold, she flung up her hand in a military salute.

"Hail, my masters," she cried in Arabic. "Would you believe it? but just now I was nearly robbed, before your windows, of merchandise that cost me thirty ounces."

"Be good enough to speak French," said the commandant; "it is the etiquette of the office."

"And to you?" exclaimed Mirza, in the speech of Paris, "to you, who speak such charming Arabic. It was only last week, the evening you did me the honor of supping with me, that Miriam—perhaps you will pay her the compliment of remembering her—the little girl who played and danced for you, and who, when you were going, hooked on your sword for you, and gave you a light from her cigarette?—well, Miriam said, when you were gone, 'It is a pity the gracious commandant speaks any language save Arabic, he speaks that so convincingly.' What could you have whispered to her, Monsieur le Commandant, as you left my poor house?"

The commandant moved nervously in his chair and glanced out of the corner of his eye at the lawyer, who had resumed his cards. Reassured by the apparent abstraction of his friend, the commandant gathered himself and essayed a pleasantry.

"I told her," he said, "that if she lived to be twice her age, she might be half as beautiful as you."

Mirza made an exaggerated courtesy and threw a mocking kiss from her finger-tips. "I thought," she said, "that a woman's age was something that no well-bred Frenchman would speak of." Then she drew herself up and her face, from mocking, became hard and cruel.

"I know," she said, slowly, "that I am old. I am eight-and-twenty. I was a wife at twelve, and a mother at thirteen. Such matters are ordered differently here, Monsieur. A girl is a woman before she has had any childhood. I married Ilderhim. Of course, I had never seen him until we stood before the cadi. I had the misfortune to bear him a daughter, and he cursed me. When I was fourteen, a Russian Grand Duke came to Biskra and my husband sold me to him. I refused to submit myself. Then Ilderhim beat me and turned me out of his house. You understand, Monsieur le Commandant, that under our blessed religion a man may have as many wives as he chooses and may divorce them when he chooses. Well, there I was, without a husband, without a home, without my child, and I passed the night in the arcades, among the camels. The next morning I went to the hotel and asked for the Grand Duke. 'Monsieur,' I said to him, 'I am Mirza. I would not *sell* myself to you, but if you will take me as a gift, behold, here am I.' He took me to Paris, to Vienna, to St. Petersburg. For a year he did not tire of me. That was a long time for a savage to amuse a Grand Duke, was it not? Then one day he gave me money, bade me keep the jewels he had given me, and sent me back to Biskra. Since then I have been, first a dancing-girl, and then, the mother of them all. I have never given the authorities any trouble. I have observed the laws of France. What will the laws of France do for me?" and she handed to the commandant the invoice which Abdullah had brought with his freight.

The commandant read the paper and his face grew troubled.

"Chancellor," he said, "is this binding?"

The lawyer read the paper twice. "Yes," he said, "it is a mere hiring; it is not a sale. I don't see how we can interfere."

"Mirza," said the commandant, "it seems that you have a good contract, under Moslem law."

"Excellent," cried the *oukil*, rubbing his hands.

"Silence," thundered the commandant. "Speak French, and that only when you are spoken to. Abdullah, have you anything which you wish to say to me?"

Abdullah bent and whispered in the ear of the girl who sat trembling; then he stepped forward.

"Monsieur le Commandant," he said, "will you have the kindness to read this?" and he held out a paper. It was yellow with age and of quarto size and twice folded. The commandant took it, unfolded it, and read aloud, "*The grace of our Lord Jesus Christ be with you all. Amen.*"

"Why, this is the last page of a Bible," he said.

"I do not know," said Abdullah. "He tore it from a book upon his table. It was the only paper that he had. Upon the other side is writing."

The commandant reversed the paper and again read:

THIS is to Certify that on the nineteenth day of February, 187-, in the Oasis of Zama, in the Great Sahara, having first baptized them, I did unite in marriage Philip (formerly Abdullah) and Marie (formerly Nicha), in accordance with the rites of our holy Church.

>   JOSEPH,
>   *Who Keeps Goats.*
>
> *Witness,*
>   his
> Ali, *the son of Ali* X
>   mark
>
>   her
> ZINA, *parentage unknown* X
>   mark

"Ah, ha," exclaimed the lawyer, "this changes the complexion of affairs," and he threw the cards upon the floor. "I could swear to Joseph's handwriting, I have his IOU's, but as I am now sitting as a magistrate, I cannot swear to anything. Where are the witnesses, Abdullah?"

"With the camels, across the square," said Abdullah; "if you will permit the corporal to go for them—"

"Pardon," said the *oukil*; "if I am permitted to speak I can save you the trouble. We admit all that the goatherd certifies."

"Then," said the chancellor, "you admit yourselves out of court, since, if one Christian marries another, the law of France obtains, and this contract which Mirza produces is abhorrent to the law of France, being immoral."

"Pardon," said the *oukil*. "In every word you speak I recognize my master, but is it not possible that my master may nod? As one of a conquered people, I have studied the code of my conqueror. It is true that a religious ceremony has been performed here, but how about the civil marriage which, as I read the French code, is absolutely necessary?"

The lawyer sat silent. Then he put out his hand. "My friend," he said, "I have done you a great wrong. I have looked upon you as a mere religionist. It seems that you are a student. You remind me of my duty. I, as the chief legal officer of this colony, should marry these people at once. Thank you many times for reminding me."

"Pardon," said the *oukil*, "but if I have read the laws of France aright, there cannot be a civil marriage without the consent of the parents."

"My friend," said the lawyer, "will you place me doubly in your debt by shaking hands with me a second time? If you were to exchange your green turban for the silk hat of the boulevards, your photograph would soon be in the shops. You know my law much better than I know yours, and I shake hands with you intellectually, not socially. Who is your father, Abdullah?" he asked.

"I do not know his name," answered Abdullah; "he was a camel-driver of the Sahara."

"And your mother?" asked the lawyer.

"How can one, born as I, know his mother?" replied Abdullah.

"And you," said the lawyer, turning to Nicha, "who is your father?"

"Ilderhim of El Merb," she answered.

"And your mother?" asked the lawyer.

"She died before I can remember."

"Her father, Ilderhim," said the *oukil*, "signs the invoice which you have read. He does not consent."

"He is nobody," said the lawyer. "He was banished from Algeria years ago. It is as though he had never existed."

"I had overlooked that," said the *oukil*, and then he added, "As the mistake this time is mine, perhaps you will again shake hands."

"No," said the lawyer; "I pay penance only when I am in the wrong."

The *oukil* bowed low, but when he drew himself up to his full height there was murder in his eye.

"Well," said the commandant, "what is the solution?"

"I advise you," said the lawyer, "that this contract comes under the law of France and is void, because it is immoral and opposed to public policy. It comes under the law of France because the young woman is a Christian and has married a Christian. The religious marriage is complete. The civil marriage is only delayed that the young woman may present proofs of her mother's death. Her father is already civilly dead."

"Mirza," said the commandant, "do you hear?"

"Yes," she said, "I hear, and, being a woman, I am accustomed to such decisions. I pay thirty ounces to Ilderhim for two years' hire of a girl. The girl turns Christian and I lose the thirty ounces."

"Not so," said Abdullah; "they are here," and he placed a bag upon the commandant's table.

"Take it," said Mirza; and she tossed it to the *oukil*.

"To make his contract good," she continued, "Ilderhim, my former husband, pays sixteen or seventeen ounces' freight on the girl and her maid. The girl turns Christian. Who loses the freight?"

"I," said Abdullah, and he placed another bag upon the table.

"Take it," said Mirza, and the *oukil* grasped it.

"Let us see this girl who has kept us all up so late," said Mirza, and she strode over to Nicha. Abdullah put out his hand to keep her off.

"You've won," she said; "why be disagreeable? Let us see what you have gained and I have lost," and she stripped the veil and the outer garment from the girl, who sat passive. When the veil and the burnoose fell, the beauty of the girl filled the room as would a perfume.

The commandant and the lawyer sat speechless, gazing. The *oukil* wrung his hands and exclaimed: "What have we lost!" Abdullah stood, proud and happy. The corporal at the door shifted his feet and rattled his side-arms, and Mirza laughed. Then she stepped back a pace; the laughter died upon her lips, and her hands flew to her bosom.

"Little one," she said, "the life you would have lived with me would not have been so hard when one remembers what the life of woman is, at best. It is to amuse, to serve, to obey. You are too young to understand. You are, perhaps, fourteen?"

"Yes," said Nicha.

"When I was fourteen," said Mirza, "I too was beautiful; at least my husband and my mirror told me so. There is something in your face that reminds me of the face I used to see in my glass, but when one grows old, and I am eight-and-twenty, one is sure to see resemblances that do not exist. How prettily they have dressed you! Did Ilderhim, your father, give you these silks and these emeralds?"

"Yes," said Nicha.

"If you are hoping to be a good wife," said Mirza, "you must not think too much of silks and jewels. When I was in Paris, with the Grand Duke, I noticed that the women who had sold themselves had taken their pay in pearls and diamonds. The honest women went more soberly. I see you are of the old tribe—the tribe of Ouled Nail. Let me see your name."

She raised the filigree medallion that hung upon Nicha's upper arm. She looked at the tattooed crest, started, drew her hand across her eyes, looked again, and fell to trembling. She stood a moment, swaying, and then she staggered to the commandant's table. She rested one hand upon it and with the other she began playing with Ali's knife. Her face was gray but her lips were pitifully smiling.

"Monsieur the Chancellor," she said, each word a sob, "you need no longer delay the civil marriage.—I consent to it,—This is my daughter.—It seems," she added, in a whisper, "that Allah has not altogether forgotten me.—He has saved my child from me." And with an exceeding bitter cry she went out.

Milton Keynes UK
Ingram Content Group UK Ltd.
UKHW031147311024
450535UK00004B/129